Wales in *Vanity Fair*

Wales in *Vanity Fair*

A Show of Cartoons by 'Ape', 'Spy' and Other Artists of Welsh Personalities of the Victorian Age

by David Dykes

Amgueddfa Genedlaethol Cymru
National Museum of Wales
Cardiff 1989

Production: Hywel G. Rees
Design: Alan Evans, Barry
Typesetting: Megaron, Cardiff
Type: Plantin
Photography: National Museum of Wales
Paper: matt silk 135 gsm
Printing: South Western Printers, Caerphilly

ISBN 0 7200 0327 X

The National Museum of Wales is grateful to
Lloyd's Bank PLC and to the Friends of the
National Museum for their financial
assistance towards this publication

Cover illustration: Henry Richard by 'Spy'.
Vanity Fair 4 September 1880

Contents

O wad some Pòw'r the giftie gie us
To see oursels as others see us!

Robert Burns
To a Louse

The most faithful mirror and record of
representative men and the spirit of
their time will be sought and found in
Vanity Fair.

Sir Leslie Ward
Forty Years of 'Spy'

Preface

The inheritance, at a very early age, of some yellowed scraps of an old magazine and, much more importantly at the time, of the colourful cartoon portraits that went with them first sparked off such interest as I have in history. The funny caricatures – 'funny' in both the primary meanings of that word – evoked for a seven year old an age completely alien to his own limited experience and one totally beyond true recall except, perhaps, through the received knowledge of his parents. The tattered pages of *Vanity Fair* – since this, I found out long afterwards, was the source of these crumbling sheets of newsprint – were soon discarded by a youngster far more intrigued by the cartoons they accompanied than the commentaries of 'Jehu Junior' which in any case he could not understand.

The treasured cartoons gradually helped to bring about some glimmering understanding of the time span of the past. They brought home, too, the eventual realisation that while the past was 'a foreign country' where 'they do things differently'[1] it was inhabited by real people with whom one could develop an identity. People not unlike those past celebrities of our own town whom my mother would habitually refer to as 'pieces of Swansea China': indeed, as I was soon to discover, one of my favourite characters – described cryptically, it seemed, as a 'wet Quaker' – eccentric and endearingly admirable – was in reality just such a rare piece of Swansea China.

As time passed the cartoons of *Vanity Fair* were increasingly to give life to my chosen period of history – the so-called Victorian age – and, through their topicality and immediacy, and, in some instances, through their very ephemerality – they were to bring flesh and blood to the actors who occupied the stage of that vigorous and dynamic epoch.

For nearly half a century, from 1868 to 1914 *Vanity Fair*, week by week, held up a mirror to the political and social life of Britain. As 'Spy', its most famous cartoonist, was to say 'When the history of the Victorian Era comes to be written in true perspective the most faithful mirror and record of representative men and the spirit of the times will be sought and found in *Vanity Fair*'[2]. Leslie Ward's self-justifying words are, of course, an exaggeration and represent a partial view: the magazine was aimed primarily at established society and it reflected the interests and, to a degree, the political sympathies of its readership. Nevertheless, although *Vanity Fair*'s broad approach was naturally of a conservative bent it did somehow convey the essence of informed society's perception of affairs generally. Because the magazine viewed the political and social 'vanities' of the age with a rheumy, but never malign, eye, and was ever-ready to burlesque even the innermost circles of its audience, it achieved that degree of acceptability in its own genteel age that has been accorded since only to the more acerbic *Private Eye*.

There was thus much truth in its presentation of the second half of Victoria's reign. Although its significance would naturally have been quite lost on contemporaries the year of *Vanity Fair*'s foundation was virtually the mid-point of that reign – and, especially through its cartoons and the accompanying commentaries, *Vanity Fair* did serve to mirror, sometimes acutely, the tremendous transformation that was taking place in Britain. In 1897 Lord Salisbury could eulogise the Queen as having 'bridged over that great interval which separates old England from new England'[3]. But the changes that had taken place between 1868 and the Diamond Jubilee were far greater and achieved at far greater pace than those of the previous thirty-odd years. Society, industry, agriculture, religious and scientific ideas, politics all seemed to be in a continuous state of flux. The years of *Vanity Fair* were years of unparalleled change and future shock. In Britain, industrial and demographic change on a scale hardly conceived of even by contemporaries, far reaching political reform leading to the creation of an urban democracy, the first vestiges of a popular educational system, the professional-isation of some of the most hallowed regions of established society, the efflorescence of science and its unshackling from an atavistic past, bitter religious controversy: in Europe, the final disruption of the old balance of power that had existed since the defeat of Napoleon, the rise of new nation states and the jockeying for power and influence on a world stage that was to lead remorselessly to the catastrophe of 1914. A half century that began with all the confidence of unquestionable 'improvement' and progress but developed increasingly a growing note of doubt. Nowhere is this better seen than in a comparison between the magazine's first cartoon of a self-confident Disraeli and its very last of a sick and broken Joseph Chamberlain bearing all the woes of the world.

The decades of *Vanity Fair* were also years of great change and debate in Wales: the immense thrust of industrial development, the growth of Nonconformity and of religious controversy that was to result in the eventual disestablishment of the Church, the land question culminating in the Carrington Commission enquiry of 1891, the development of a middle class, which given political power in 1867, in due course changed dramatically the balance of political influence in Wales, and, by no means unconnected, the flowering of that Welsh cultural renaissance which was to give to the nation its great institutions, the University, the National Library and the National Museum.

Vanity Fair, it must be remembered though, was a metropolitan magazine and the mirror that it held up reflected the scene as viewed from London or Westminster. To many of those at the centre of power Wales was still a remote country, a mysterious world shrouded yet in romantic mists and peopled by a race which spoke a foreign tongue. *Vanity Fair* took no special or direct interest in Wales as such except when the problems of the Principality impinged on what were credited as more central 'imperial' issues. Therefore, many of those figures who played such a significant role within Wales at the time were ignored unless they captured the eye of Westminster or performed also on the British national scene. Nonetheless, through the 'weekly show of political and literary wares' a great deal can still be said about Wales at this time; this is what we have tried to do in this short work.

This book was written as an accompaniment to a similarly entitled exhibition which opened at the Main Building of the National Museum of Wales in Cardiff on 13 December 1988 and was subsequently mounted at other venues in the Principality. Neither the book nor the exhibition would have been possible but for the help and support of a number of friends and colleagues in the Museum and in other sister institutions. I owe a particular debt of gratitude to Professor Glanmor Williams who not only opened the original exhibition but who read the text of the book and rescued me from a variety of solecisms, both literary and factual. Thanks are due, too, to my colleagues Dr. Christine Johnson who shouldered so much of the weight unavoidable in mounting even a simple exhibition, to Hywel Rees and Ian Kane for their artistic flair and imaginative preparation of both book and exhibition, to Eric Broadbent and Kevin Thomas for their meticulous photography, to Paul Rees for so effectively mounting all the cartoons exhibited and to Dr. Dafydd Roberts and Dr. Bill Jones for advising on historical queries. The Librarian of the National Museum, John Kenyon, as ever, has been assiduous in searching out recondite biographies for me: my thanks are due to him and also to the staff of the London Library. Finally, my thanks are due to Mrs. Moira Curtis, my secretary, and Mrs. Gwyneth Tobin who typed the text of the present volume from an almost indecipherable manuscript.

The majority of the cartoons included in the exhibition and illustrated here come from a private collection while those illustrated on pp. 11, 13, 14 top, 44, 49, 56 and 72 are from the collections of the National Museum of Wales. To the following I owe thanks for lending cartoons and other works and for permitting them to be illustrated in this book: The Trustees of the British Museum (p. 14 bottom); the President and Council of the Royal Institution of South Wales (and particularly Dr. David Painting and Miss Betty Nelmes)(pp. 79 and 83); and the Council and Librarian of the National Library of Wales (pp. 43, 50, 55, 59, 86, 89 and 92).

18 December 1988   David Dykes

[1]   The opening words of *The Go Between* by L. P. Hartley: 'The past is a foreign country: they do things differently there'.
[2]   Leslie Ward, *Forty Years of 'Spy'* (London 1915), p. 331.
[3]   Quoted in Donald Read, *England 1868-1914* (London 1979), p. 3.

Introduction

The Origins of Caricature

For centuries visual satire has played a key role in political and social commentary. From the time of the Reformation, certainly, the crude imagery of the polemical print proved a potent – and cruel – weapon in the satirist's reduction of religious dogma and political pretension to the level of contempt or ridicule. There is, however, little evidence of the use of personal caricature – the comic distortion of some salient feature of an individual's person or dress – in these clumsy and crude pictorial satires much before the beginning of the seventeenth century. Indeed, even the superb baroque prints of the Dutch artist – engravers of the latter part of the seventeenth and the earlier years of the eighteenth century depended more on allegory and emblem than on caricature.

In its modern recognisable form the caricature seems to have originated from the Italian studios of Agostino and Annibale Carracci, the latter best known to the art historian as the master of the 'grand manner'. Although his caricatures are unknown today it is Annibale Carracci (1560-1609) who is credited as being the inventor of the form. To him the essence of the portrait caricature lay in the recognition that the deliberate exaggeration or distortion of even a single personal feature could serve not to destroy the likeness of an individual but rather to transform him so that his true character could be strikingly captured in a new light. In his defence of caricature as a counterpart to the ideal Annibale Carracci saw

> the caricaturist's task [as being] exactly the same as the classical artist's. Both see the lasting truth beneath the surface of mere outward appearance. Both try to help nature to accomplish its plan. The one may strive to visualise the perfect form and to realise it in his work, the other to grasp the perfect deformity, and thus reveal the very essence of a personality. A good caricature, like every work of art, is more true to life than reality itself[1].

Originally the caricature was viewed as a harmless pastime for leisure hours, a personal diversion among friends. And it soon achieved fashionable status in Italian *dilettanti* circles where the gentle mockery of the caricature became accepted as a form of flattery. In the early years of the eighteenth century, the artist Pier Leone Ghezzi (1674-1755) was the first to receive popular acclaim – and perhaps not a modicum of his living – for

Joseph Henry of Straffon, Count Kildare, *c.1750, by Pier Leone Ghezzi.*

his vivid but rather genteel caricatures, especially of the many art lovers who flocked to Rome and in particular its English colony. But caricature at this time remained essentially an Italian art form. Although the genre was certainly not unknown in England before, it was not until 1744 that it was introduced to a wider English audience by Arthur Pond, the painter and engraver, with the publication of his set of etchings of caricatures by Ghezzi and other Italian artists. These etchings were of considerable importance in encouraging an interest in caricature in England. Nevertheless, the satirical prints of the gusty political broadsheets, lampooning government and establishment, which flooded London in the first half of the eighteenth century were, in most instances, still very much the heirs to the crude pictorial libels of earlier polemical propaganda although in some instances a more sophisticated genre was developing.

William Hogarth (b.1697) dominated this whole period until his death in 1764, his career spanning the early vogue of the political satire from the emblematic designs of the Dutch artist-engravers to the rise of the cheap coloured print. Trained originally as an engraver Hogarth was a versatile artist who, lacking sufficient of the fickle favour of aristocratic patrons for traditional portraits and conversation-pieces, suffered great hardship in his early life. He eventually came into his own through the painting and engraving of what he described as 'modern moral subjects' where, adapting the exalted historical style to the contemporary social scene, he could, through the narrative extension of the dramatic conversation-piece, 'arrest the thoughtless in their hasty steps to evil [and] . . . confirm the prudent in their steady march towards good'.[2] In his individual plates such as *Gin Lane* and *Beer Street* and his celebrated sets of narrative prints like *The Rake's Progress* and *Marriage à la Mode* he exposed hypocrisy and human fallibility through the emotional earthiness and complex symbolism of his social tableaux and created a body of painting to rival the greatest satiric writing of the Augustan Age.

The Bench, *1758–1764, by William Hogarth. The caption sets out the artist's distinction between* Character, *which renders nature with absolute fidelity, and* Caricatura *whose effect depends on the distortion of physical appearance. The central figure is Sir John Willes, the Lord Chief Justice. Hogarth was still working on this plate the day before his death.*

Hogarth welded together the satiric tradition of the Dutch artist-engravers and 'that modern fashion, caricature' as he described it in his characteristically dismissive way. Hogarth, it must be stressed, despised the Italian caricature tradition as frivolous and mere skit. He saw himself rather as a student of character working on a far more elevated intellectual plane. To him the depicture of *character* required absolute fidelity to one's subject while *caricature*, on the other hand, depended upon the distortion of appearance. Nevertheless, through his social satire Hogarth established caricature in England and it is not for nothing that he has been accorded the title of the 'father of English caricature'. Hogarth engraved few overtly *political* satires but in his etching of John Wilkes, for example, the two traditions of broadside propaganda and classical caricature are completely brought together, though to Hogarth himself the result was much more a faithful representation of a dissolute scoundrel than any form of caricature.

John Wilkes, *1763, by William Hogarth.*

Even though it was still regarded as a sophisticated joke for the virtuosi the pure classic Italian style of caricature had established itself in England and, through the work of George, first Marquis Townshend (1724-1807), in the second half of the eighteenth century it emerged as a political weapon. Credited by Horace Walpole as the inventor of the political portrait caricature, Townshend clearly shows through his drawings and etchings the influence of the Italian style with its distortion of physical characteristic. An amateur, the naive crudity of his malicious and spiteful cartoons popularised an essentially private diversion into an almost public craze for the drawing of caricatures. To a great extent Townshend was to shape the future development of the caricature in England over the next half century or more. Even the professional artist chose to adopt the crudity of the amateur at the expense of artistic form and design. And the 'Golden Age' of the political and social pictorial satire from, say, 1780 to 1830 is marked by a mass of productions which gained in strength and public esteem from their very crudeness and, indeed, ribaldry which reflected the popular taste of the day.

What seems now to have been an almost insatiable appetite for the titillating gossip of social scandal and political faction, stimulated by a far from uninhibited press, created, through popular exhibition and print-shop, a ready market for the 'low art' of the caricature. And, indeed, for its voguish and more respectable counterpoint the portrait print. In essence both caricature and portrait print owed their existence to the public's perception of individual *reputation*: the one a cynical detraction, the other a sublime idealisation seen in its highest form in the portraits of a Gainsborough or a Reynolds. By now the word *caricature* had come into common usage and took on its modern meaning – to ridicule and to reprove through distortion.

The perfection of political caricature as a distinctive genre owes much to Townshend's later followers, particularly James Gillray (1757-1815) who was the acknowledged master of the pictorial satire in this period. Gillray in his coarse and unbridled way concentrates on the individual and his cartoons are of a more incisively subjective and personal nature than are the iconographic cartoons of Hogarth. Overshadowing his contemporaries, Gillray was of prime influence in the development of the caricature and fashioned the approach to the modern political cartoonist's art. The old devices of emblematic symbolism and abusive label were still employed but personal caricature and immediacy of subject were much more central to his cartoon. The portraiture was distilled, too, so that political personalities were reduced to a simple and readily recognisable stereotype concentrating on and distorting a single characteristic physical feature – Pitt's roseate face or gimlet nose, Napoleon's saturnine features or dwarfish stature – while the ephemeral nature of his subjects inculcated a vivid directness – devices that are still used at the present day.

The Table's Turned *(William Pitt)*, *1797, by James Gillray. The cartoon marks the abortive French landing at Carreg Wastad and Sir John Jervis's victory at Cape St. Vincent in 1797.*

The Hogarthian influence did not disappear completely as Thomas Rowlandson (1757-1827) – and amateur imitators like the London merchant John Nixon (d.1818) – continued the tradition of social satire mocking the affectations and pretensions of respectable society in terms of generalised types embodying human vice or physical beauty or deformity.

By the 1820s the output of coloured political prints had become intense, rising to a crescendo at the end of the decade in the midst of civil disturbance and the agitation for Reform. But the coarse, licentious tradition was fast coming to an end. As Britain passed through the 1830s the social climate was changing and the savagery and ribaldry of the explicit satirical cartoon was rapidly losing its popularity. William Heath (*c*. 1795-1840)

The Artist in Wales, *1799, by Thomas Rowlandson. The artist depicted is supposed to be Henry Wigstead the caricaturist.*

The Market Square, Swansea, *1799, by John Nixon.*

was, perhaps, the last major figure in a long tradition. His gift for the vivid recreation of a political figure reflected Gillray who, however, was already being regarded as 'a caterpillar on the green leaf of reputation'.[3] Public attitude was becoming more refined and the all too often indelicate single sheet engraving was giving way to the muted humorous illustration of newspaper and magazine circumscribed by the even-handed requirements of an editorial board.

Robertena Peelena the Maid of All Work *(Sir Robert Peel)*, *1829, by William Heath.*

Gillray and Rowlandson had no equals abroad but as the English rejected the explicit style of the Georgian cartoonists in favour of a more decorous style befitting the 'proper' sensibilities and moral earnestness of the coming Victorian generations, the satirical caricature moved to France to re-appear in 1830 in the comic weekly *La Caricature* and, later, in the daily *Charivari* published by Charles Philipon (1806-1862). A caricaturist of ability and an enterprising publisher, Philipon understood the essence of the successful caricature and the interplay between the visual and the verbal joke. He captured the public imagination with his sensational court justification of his representation of King Louis-Philippe as a pear (pear = poire = dimwit).

Philipon's great contribution to the development of the caricature was the discovery of new talent, promoting the work of Grandville, Doré and the great master Daumier and in particular the development of the *portrait-chargé* or 'distorted likeness' as a weapon of visual satire. Daumier perfected the lithographed *portrait-chargé* and, by the 1860s, especially from the hands of artists like 'André Gill', it had become a feature of some ferocity in French political satire.

The launching of *Punch* in 1842 – significantly subtitled 'the London Charivari' – institutionalised the tradition of the English humorous cartoon. But although *Punch* frequently used the *portrait-chargé* in its political set pieces – Napoleon III for example – the strength of its cartoons came to lie less upon ideas than upon draughtsmanship and more upon humour than on caricature. The magazine's cartoon style was essentially narrative and the humour was often derived more from the illustration of a joke than vice versa.

The mood of conservatism and the high tone of refined respectability of the middle and upper reaches of Victorian society created a social climate that was ripe for the re-emergence of the classic form of caricature. The portrait caricatures that were to appear in *Vanity Fair* from 1869 were more subtle and far more closely attuned to middle class Victorian attitudes than the licentious and explicit Georgian cartoons or indeed the *portraits-chargés* that had emerged in France. More on a plane with Hogarthian values they set forth to bring out personality and character rather than to destroy reputation. Thomas Gibson Bowles, the founder of *Vanity Fair*, fully understood the *raison d'être* of the genteel classical portrait caricature of the Ghezzi genre and realised its potential when searching for an alternative mode of social and political satirical illustration to rival the *Punch* cartoons. Perhaps of more immediate influence were the caricature portraits that Daniel Maclise – under the *nom de crayon* of 'Alfred Croquis' – had contributed to *Frazer's Magazine* thirty years before. These elegant and slightly-mocking sketches had been the most popular single feature of the magazine and had remained collector's pieces for years afterwards.

Charles Dickens, 1861, by 'Andre Gill'.

Thomas Carlyle, 1833, by Daniel Maclise for Fraser's Magazine.

The essence of Bowles' new magazine was to mirror Victorian values and it was therefore natural that a key element in this would be the reflection of the Victorians' obsession with the cult of personality. To Bowles the aim of the caricature was to satirise by exaggerating the physical characteristics and mannerisms of eminent men and so to portray them 'not as they would be but as they are'. Although a great many of the *Vanity Fair* caricatures – especially in later years – were only trifling in their mockery there is an underlying insight and innuendo to the earliest in particular which, when taken in conjunction with the accompanying biographical sketches of 'Jehu Junior', for twenty years the *nom de plume* of Bowles himself, readily explain how they achieved their purpose of unmasking pretensions in a polite age. The very absence of the savagery and indelicacy of a Gillray or a Rowlandson was the secret of their success. The mockery was sufficiently subtle to appeal to middle-class Victorians without offending their sensibilities by appearing to be over-critical of those late-Victorian values which dictated respect for Empire and the establishment.

The caricatures were to retain their appeal throughout the life of *Vanity Fair*, but the very high standards set by the early artists – Pellegrini, Tissot and the young Leslie Ward – were rarely recaptured after the 1890s even by Ward himself and with one or two notable exceptions – Max Beerbohm is an outstanding case – the caricatures tended to degenerate into social portraits produced to a standardised formula conditioned, no doubt, by the development of popular portrait photography. In the magazine's final decade before the First World War it was even suggested – with evident truth – that some subjects were paying for their inclusion in *Vanity Fair*.

It is one of the quirks of history that while social and political commentators and cartoonists often achieve great contemporary public acclaim only rarely do their wit and humour transcend their own generation. By their very nature political and social jokes are ephemeral and are not designed to stand the test of time. The *Vanity Fair* caricatures have, however, retained their public appeal. While *Vanity Fair* itself and Bowles, its founder, and many of the once notable and perhaps formidable personalities who appeared in portrait caricature week by week are as forgotten as yesterday's news, the caricatures themselves live on. They live on as parodies of the older establishment standards of a byegone age for a public brought up on *Vanity Fair*'s nearest successor, *Private Eye*. More importantly, they live on because, at their best, they are brilliant examples of the caricaturist's art and bring home to us, through the eyes of contemporaries the eminent or *soi-disant* eminent of the day. And this is a view that must colour our perspective of the values both of subject and commentator and, indeed, of the whole later Victorian Age.

Vanity Fair: A Weekly Show of Political, Social and Literary Wares

For over half a century, from its launch in 1868 to its eventual demise in 1914, *Vanity Fair* was the leading and unrivalled Society magazine of the day – reflecting and influencing the tastes, opinions and prejudices of the Victorian and Edwardian establishment.

As originally conceived by its founder, Thomas Gibson Bowles, *Vanity Fair* was never intended to be a purely frivolous journal devoted simply to the amusement of the social set. Certainly it was expected to amuse – through its predictable mixture of serialised novels, fictionalised letters column and above all through its word-games and contests – but there was also an underlying serious intention to inform and comment. This thread runs through all the regular features from the accounts of the progress of the 'season' to the informed literary and theatrical reviews, the financial and business advice and the commentaries on domestic and world-wide political affairs. As the magazine developed over the years, however, it has to be admitted that the society news and gossip columns came to dominate and that the political and overseas news tended to become discussed more in terms of personalities than issues. But this was for the future.

Polished, urbane and sophisticated in its prose, especially in the years of Bowles's direction, the magazine's weekly news columns and often its features were written from a staunchly Conservative and Imperialist point of view, and *Vanity Fair* could always be relied upon to defend the Empire, the Established Church and the accepted order of the English social system. Nevertheless, however much *Vanity Fair*, and indeed Bowles, may have sought to support and echo Conservative policies, values and prejudices, no cow was too sacred to be spared irreverent and iconoclastic criticism. While Gladstone was inevitably suspect and radicals were beyond the pale, even Bowles's hero, Disraeli, was not immune from criticism: indeed, no individual or institution was.

Thomas Gibson Bowles by 'Spy', Vanity Fair *13 July 1889*.

Vanity Fair was essentially the product of the vision of one man, Thomas Gibson Bowles (1842-1922), its owner-editor for the first twenty years of the magazine's existence. Bowles was the natural son of Thomas Milner Gibson, a rich and prominent Cobdenite Liberal, whose wife, Susanna Arethusa, was an accomplished hostess of influence in her own right. Her dazzling salons, attended by the leading literary and political lions of the day, were the scene not only of impassioned political debate and literary criticism but also of amateur theatricals and, not least, of spiritualist seances. Mrs. Milner Gibson took her husband's illegitimate son into her own home and brought him up as a member of the family. An unrivalled opportunity was thus given to the young Bowles to meet the literary and political personalities, the fashionable bohemians and the exiled patriots who thronged Mrs. Milner Gibson's drawing room. At the age of nineteen Bowles took up a clerkship in the Inland Revenue due, no doubt, to his father's influence as President of the Board of Trade in Palmerston's second administration. His private means, though, allowed him to play the part of a young man about town which he used to advantage: contributions to the *Morning Post* (the editor Algernon Borthwick – and a formative influence in Bowles's early years – was an habitué of Mrs. Milner Gibson's salons), amateur theatricals, playwriting and involvement in a variety of ephemeral theatrical or satirical magazines such as *The Owl*, *The Glow Worm* and *The Tomahawk* aroused and sustained his literary aspirations. By the age of twenty-seven Bowles felt experienced enough to float and manage a magazine of his own.

In launching *Vanity Fair*, which first appeared on 7 November 1868, Bowles was dependent on the support of a number of friends from among the smart set. He started the magazine with no more than £200 – a modest sum for such a venture even for those days. Half of the capital was supplied by Colonel Frederick Burnaby, a cavalry man and an adventurer whose exploits would have done credit to the greatest hero of the *Boys' Own Paper*. Burnaby, it is said, contributed the magazine's title from Thackeray and its subtitle – 'We buy the Truth' – from Bunyan. Burnaby was a heavy swell and a crony of the Prince of Wales who was credited with some financial involvement in the magazine. Although this was unlikely, Lord Carrington, a close associate of the Prince in those days and the original 'Champagne Charlie', may well have been intimately associated with *Vanity Fair* in its formative years.

Whatever the financial assistance of others Bowles remained very much the proprietor and editor. And in the early days, certainly, he wrote most of the columns himself under the pseudonyms of 'Jehu Junior', 'Blanc Bec', 'Auditor', 'Choker' and 'Pantagruel'.

Frederick Burnaby by 'Spy', Vanity Fair *2 December 1876.*

Lord Carrington by 'Ape', Vanity Fair *7 February 1874.*

The Golden Age of 'Ape' and 'Spy': Pictorial Wares of an Entirely Novel Character

The first few weeks of the new magazine were not easy because there was stiff opposition from other established society journals and the funding of *Vanity Fair* was at a dangerously low level. Then in January 1869 Bowles announced that he would be introducing into the magazine 'some Pictorial Wares of an entirely novel character'. The first of these wares, a full-page coloured *portrait-chargé* of Disraeli as seen through the eyes of the Italian artist Carlo Pellegrini, under the *nom de crayon* of 'Singe' – later anglicised to 'Ape' –, appeared in the issue of *Vanity Fair* for 30 January 1869. Its success was instantaneous, the issue was a sell-out and was still being reprinted months later. The introduction of the portrait caricature, produced through the relatively new process of chromolithography, was a stroke of genius and assured not only the immediate viability but also the longer term prosperity of *Vanity Fair*.

Chemical printing or lithography had been invented by Aloys Senefelder in 1798, and although introduced to London in 1801, it was not until 1817 that it was established by Rudolf Ackermann as a fine art. It was in France, however, in the 1830s, that lithography was to be initially employed in the production of caricatures in the publications of Charles Philipon. Philipon was himself a lithographer, and adapted the technique for producing caricatures, but it was through the sensitive artistry of Daumier that its true potential was revealed. The most important advance for the caricature had been Senefelder's invention of transfer paper. This allowed the artist's original drawing to be transferred directly to the lithographic plate without the artist having to make a reverse copy of the drawing. The quality of transfer paper was greatly improved in 1868 and this new refinement enhanced the quality of the reproduction of the *Vanity Fair* caricatures.

The invention of chromolithography (the printing of lithographs in colour from several different plates) has also been attributed to Senefelder. But the process was never satisfactory until refined techniques were developed by Charles Joseph Hullmandel towards the middle of the nineteenth century which enabled chromolithography to become a commercially viable printing process.

Benjamin Disraeli by 'Singe'/'Ape', Vanity Fair *30 January 1869.*

William Ewart Gladstone by 'Singe'/'Ape', Vanity Fair *6 February 1869.*

The cartoon of Disraeli was succeeded a week later by a glowering Gladstone and, shortly, by every single member of the latter's year-old cabinet, distinguished, as the *Times* proclaimed, by an 'ability so great and so various'. Other distinguished figures of the day followed in weekly succession. In all over 2,300 cartoons were published during the magazine's lifetime, covering the whole gamut of public celebrities and popular heroes. Within a very short time, to be depicted as the victim of a *Vanity Fair* caricature had become a 'public honour no eminent man could well refuse'. Some did refuse, nevertheless, like Lewis Carroll, while others, like Anthony Trollope, reacted with choleric ill-grace on being made, by 'Spy', to look like 'an affronted Santa Claus' who had 'just lost his reindeer'.[4]

Anthony Trollope by 'Spy', Vanity Fair *5 April 1873.*

As 'Men of the Day', 'Statesmen' or 'Judges' most of the literary, scientific, political, legal, sporting and military figures of the day processed through the pages of *Vanity Fair*: Thomas Carlyle, John Ruskin, Oscar Wilde, Pasteur, Lord John Russell, Salisbury, W.G. Grace, Garnet Wolseley and Kitchener are but a few of a seemingly never-ending multitude.

And through the personification of the cartoons many of the great issues of the day were addressed: the contentious question of ritualism in the Anglican Church and the expansion of Roman Catholicism through Pusey, Newman and Manning, the debate on evolution through Darwin, Huxley and Bishop Wilberforce, and, not least, the foreboding changes in the balance of power in Europe through Tissot's incisive cartoons of Napoleon III, William I of Prussia and Bismarck.

Thomas Carlyle by 'Ape', Vanity Fair *22 October 1870.*

Charles Darwin by 'Coïdé' (James Tissot), Vanity Fair *30 September 1871.*

The *Vanity Fair* caricatures, although produced in what is thought of as a typically English idiom, were created, especially in the earlier days, by an unusually cosmopolitan group of artists. Carlo Pellegrini (1839-1889) was the first and most influential of these artists. He was the prime instigator of the re-emergence of the classic form of caricature into English satirical illustration and was the originator of the style that is recognised as 'Vanity Fair' although, and such is the benefit of survival, that it is now even more closely identified with his heir 'Spy'.

Carlo Pellegrini by 'AHM' (Arthur Marks), Vanity Fair *27 April 1889.*

Of aristocratic Italian lineage, Pellegrini began his career as an amateur caricaturist among the *beau monde* of Naples. French influence was widespread in this fashionable society but, although responsive to the style, the Neapolitan caricaturists did not adopt the highly charged atmosphere of the French *portrait-chargé*. Melchiorre Delfico's caricatures, for example, which were to have a profound influence on Pellegrini, while lacking nothing in satire, were urbane and elegant in form and it is in this tradition, the genteel Italian tradition of the classical Ghezzi, that Pellegrini found his inspiration.

Pellegrini always maintained that he arrived in London in 1864 in mysterious and impecunious circumstances, although this is very likely a romanticised myth created to embellish his Bohemian image. For however destitute his early circumstances they were destined to be short lived, as his Neapolitan charm, artistry as a caricaturist, and personal eccentricities soon ensured his adoption by London society and ultimately the patronage of the coterie of the Prince of Wales. Once established within these fashionable inner circles, it was inevitable that he should be introduced to Thomas Gibson Bowles, no doubt through the salon of the redoubtable Mrs. Milner Gibson. It remains, though, one of the oddities of fate that their long and erratic partnership should produce such a peculiarly English institution as the *Vanity Fair* caricature.

The relationship between Bowles, the sophisticated, literary man-about-town, and Pellegrini, the volatile *prima donna*, was destined to be stormy. Nevertheless, despite their frequent quarrels and estrangements, Pellegrini contributed to *Vanity Fair* from

1869 until 1889, the year of his death. Pellegrini achieved great contemporary fame for his caricatures but he was to be less successful, although fashionable, as a conventional portrait painter. His caricatures are remarkably consistent in their quality even though they span a period of almost twenty years. The single figures, rarely embellished with more than a shadow, set the mode for nearly half a century. The caricatures display a penetrating honesty that was never compromised by flattery. Max Beerbohm generously acknowledged the profound influence of 'Ape' on his own work. To Beerbohm, 'Ape' was 'by far the best caricaturist who has lived within our time'.[5] David Low, one of the most important of twentieth century cartoonists, recognised Pellegrini's genius in his ability to produce a portrait of true likeness that revealed deep insight into the projected public persona. In Low's words ' 'Ape's' caricatures represented not only what he saw but also what he knew. Most of them today look as though they were probably more like the persons they depict than were those persons themselves'.[6] To 'Ape' himself a caricature was 'a comic portrait yet with as much of a man's disposition as you can get into it'.[7] This is the sublime essence of Pellegrini's artistry, and the basis of his status as a great master of the caricature.

Pellegrini was the first and the most influential of the *Vanity Fair* caricaturists but he was not without rivals. The magazine was open to other talents that were deemed acceptable to the social milieu of its editor, especially if they also possessed the romantic attraction of being foreign. As early as September 1869 the French· society painter James Tissot, under the *nom de crayon* of 'Coïdé', launched a special series of caricatures of European royalty before he returned to Paris for the Franco-Prussian War and the Siege (where incidentally Bowles was present, too, as a correspondent for *The Morning Post*). These caricatures – probably bought in as a 'job lot' by Bowles – are the nearest approximation to the truly political cartoon in *Vanity Fair*.

William I of Prussia, later Emperor of Germany by 'Coïdé' (James Tissot), Vanity Fair *7 January 1871*.

In all, Tissot submitted sixty-two cartoons between 1869 and 1877 – the late ones subscribed 'JtJ' or 'm' – before finally leaving London to resume his career as a painter. His early cartoons, bright and lively, contrast sharply with the economical and monochromatic caricatures of Pellegrini. Tissot's training as a painter and a lithographer is clearly evident in his work. The exceptional quality of his cartoons, even by *Vanity Fair* standards, is a result of his excellent draftsmanship, an ability to work directly onto the lithography plate without the use of transfer paper, and his deep understanding of the use of colour. Adopting a style often closer to realism than to caricature, his cartoons could be devastating, like the *tours de force* of the bent and broken Napoleon III and the contrastingly confident and vigorous Bismarck. After his arrival in London in 1871 Tissot, with his usual skill, quickly adapted himself to the more gentle style of 'Ape' and his later 'English' caricatures are markedly milder in approach.

The Emperor Napoleon III of France by 'Coïdé' (*James Tissot*), Vanity Fair *4 September 1869.*

Prince Bismarck by 'Coïdé' (James Tissot), Vanity Fair *15 October 1870.*

During the lifetime of *Vanity Fair* other French artists were also associated with the magazine, but without exception, they were not of the calibre of Tissot. Nevertheless, substantial contributions were made by Theobald Chartran (1849-1907) between 1874 and 1884 and by Jean Baptiste Guth (d.1921) who produced forty-three cartoons, mainly of French personalities from 1897 to 1910. With the exception of Pellegrini, the Italian school was not particularly influential. In the 1870s Adriano Cecioni (1838-1886) and Melchiorre Delfico himself (1825-1895) were both commissioned by Bowles, but it is the caricatures of the racing fraternity, executed by Liberio Prosperi at the end of the nineteenth century, that are probably the best known.

In the face of the European tradition of caricature, the transatlantic influence on the *Vanity Fair* cartoons was, in comparison, minor. However, a number of celebrated Americans did appear in *Vanity Fair* from time to time as the victims of both 'Ape' and 'Spy'. Some of the most effective satirical caricatures in this series came from the pen of the German-American Thomas Nast (1840-1902), political cartoonist of the Civil War and of the Italian Risorgimento, and populariser of the American 'Santa Claus', who provided a particularly venomous portrait of the journalist-politician and Presidential candidate Horace Greeley.

None of these artists established themselves and, in 1873, when Bowles was actively seeking a replacement for Pellegrini, after one of their many quarrels, the twenty-two-

Horace Greeley (by Thomas Nast), Vanity Fair *20 July 1872*.

year old Leslie Ward was brought to his notice by Sir John Millais, a family friend of the Wards. In terms of his background, temperament and working methods, Leslie Ward (1851-1922) was the very antithesis of Pellegrini. Born into a family of fashionable artists, his education and connections provided him with a natural place in London society. In contrast to the extrovert and excitable Pellegrini, Ward exhibited the dry, refined wit of his milieu and always exhibited a low patronising opinion of his rival.

Lesley Ward by 'PAL' (Jean de Paleologue), Vanity Fair *23 November 1889*.

The first Ward cartoon 'Old Bones', which had been the basis of the Millais introduction, appeared in March 1873 and depicted Professor Richard Owen, the Superintendent of the Natural History Department of the British Museum and arch-enemy of Huxley in the Darwinian evolution controversy.

Richard Owen (by Lesley Ward), Vanity Fair *1 March 1873.*

Thus, with the subsequent help of Dr. Johnson's Dictionary – for the Owen cartoon was unattributed – 'Spy' was launched on a permanent career and *Vanity Fair* was set to become a national institution. The 'Spy' cartoons were to be a regular feature of *Vanity Fair* for over forty years and although Ward yearned for acceptance as a society portrait painter his devotion was to *Vanity Fair*. His caricatures were the product of lengthy and meticulous observation and thus retain an element of portraiture which is absent from Pellegrini's work, the product of lightning sketches and a highly retentive memory. Ward has also been criticised for resorting to flattery, especially in his caricatures of royalty, but many of his cartoons, in particular those of the judiciary, have a sharp, biting edge. One thinks, too, of his depiction of the unprincipled ambition evident in the character of F.E. Smith. Nevertheless, even though Max Beerbohm thought that Pellegrini's work had lost its bite before the end of the 1870s, in comparison to 'Ape', 'Spy' remains, on the whole, mild and gentlemanly, more concerned with personal foible and eccentricity than a fundamental analysis of character. The difference in style between 'Ape' and 'Spy' may well be deeply rooted. For it is possible that the penetrating insight demonstrated by Pellegrini could only have come from an outside observer. Ward, with all his advantages of belonging to the establishment, was probably less perceptive and more than a little myopic when observing the foibles of a world that was his own.

Although he became the prime caricaturist to *Vanity Fair* 'Spy' did not have the field entirely to himself and occasionally other artists were called upon. Very few became permanent, however, and most of them have disappeared into a decent obscurity. Towards the end of the *Vanity Fair* era, as the caricatures decayed into portraits, only the work of Max Beerbohm was of a quality comparable to that of 'Ape' in the early years of the magazine. The witty style of Beerbohm with its economy of line is a tribute to the influence of Pellegrini, and is a sublime example of what the *Vanity Fair* cartoon might have become if it had not succumbed to pure commercialism.

The Last Years of *Vanity Fair*

After some twenty years as the driving force behind *Vanity Fair*, Bowles began to tire of his magazine. He had developed an active interest in politics. Other ventures attracted him, too, while personal tragedy encouraged him to turn his back on the past. In 1889, therefore, Bowles sold *Vanity Fair* to Arthur H. Evans for £20,000. The general style of the publication continued under the editorship of A.G. Witherby, Oliver Fry, B. Fletcher Robinson and Frank Harris. The magazine, however, never fully recovered from the loss of Bowles. His characteristically urbane, if pungently witty, style could be only faintly captured by lesser journalists, and *Vanity Fair* slowly degenerated into little more than a gossip sheet. This downward trend was also sadly to be observed in the standard of the caricatures. Before long, Leslie Ward had become past his best, and even the penetrating pen of a 'W.A.G.' (A.G. Witherby) or the brilliancy of a Beerbohm could not save the magazine. In 1911 *Vanity Fair* was sold once more and in 1914 it was finally absorbed into *Hearth and Home*.

Vanity Fair's very last cartoon, published on 14 January 1914, a month before its own demise, was of a sick and broken Joseph Chamberlain. More truly than its artist – 'Astz' – could have realised, it tolled the passing of an era. The years of confidence that *Vanity Fair* had chronicled, the way of life that it had stood for and so often parodied were shortly to be swept away in the horrors of the Great War.

Joseph Chamberlain by 'Astz',
Vanity Fair *14 January 1914*.

1 Quoted in Ernst H. Gombrich and Ernst Kris, *Caricature* (London 1940), pp. 11-12.
2 Quoted in David Low, *British Cartoonists, Caricaturists and Comic Artists* (London 1942), p. 8
3 *The Athenaeum*, 1831, p. 633.
4 James Pope Hennessy, *Anthony Trollope* (St. Albans 1973), pp. 309-310.
5 *Max Beerbohm, Letters to Reggie Turner* (ed. Rupert Hart-Davis, London 1954), p. 297.
6 David Low, op. cit., p. 33.
7 B. Fletcher Robinson, 'Chronicles in Cartoon: A Record of Our Own Times', *The Windsor Magazine* (London 1905), p. 42.

A Selection of Pictorial Wares from Wales

The Land: Wales and Welsh Society

In the first few years of *Vanity Fair* those Englishmen who thought about Wales, including, no doubt, the majority of the magazine's metropolitan readership saw the country as a remote, romantic, still perhaps not wholly – civilised world that was mysteriously shrouded in Celtic enchantment. This was still very much the quaint image of an Ibbetson or even the picturesque perception of a Borrow barely a generation before: an awareness of Wales but an awareness of something peculiar to be patronised, something of little political consequence that in its very oddness was aberrant. Yet, peeling away the layers of romantic notion there was, of course, more than a hard core of truth. Despite the very many contacts that had developed between England and the Principality over the previous hundred years and more, through scholarship, religion and philanthropy, the growth of insular travel and, not least, the development of industrial enterprise, Wales remained apart from the main stream of the social and political life of Britain. While, governmentally, the Principality, was firmly part of the English 'system' in ways in which Scotland and Ireland were not, in cultural terms and in the pattern of its life Wales was not England and was perceived not to be so, however unwelcome this perception might be.

Matthew Arnold by 'Coïdé' (James Tissot), Vanity Fair *11 November 1871.*

Arnold fostered the concept of Wales as a country of swirling mists inhabited by 'ineffectual' Celts lost in mysticism and contrasted them with their Saxon neighbours overcome by the 'despotism of fact'. His appreciation of the value of Celtic culture and literature, nevertheless, helped to promote its study.

Wales was different in language, in social structure, and above all, perhaps, in the growing degree of its Nonconformity, which, underpinning the mass of society and its language, in the course of the nineteenth century inculcated a characteristic ethos which was to shape the political and social outlook of the nation.

In his polemical tracts Henry Richard could describe the years before 1868 – that mythic year of 'national awakening' – as years of 'feudalism', as a time of political subjection when no question relating to Wales occupied the attention of Parliament. Already, though, even in these years of 'stagnation', a sea-change was beginning to take place which was to create the basis for the religious passion, the political achievement and the educational progress that were the keynotes of the latter part of the century and were to make so much impact upon the national stage. The continuing use of the Welsh language in most parts of Wales before the development of a state education system after 1870 was stimulated by the grass-roots growth of Nonconformity and the spread of chapel and Sunday school. In turn, the chapel and Nonconformity's own popular press, were to highlight the grievances of dissent and the associated inequalities of Welsh society and to foster that nationwide radicalism which was to make national issues of tithes, disestablishment, burial laws and home rule and to spawn a new breed of politician like Samuel Evans, Tom Ellis, and Lloyd George.

Nevertheless, although it might have been politically advantageous to see Wales as stagnant, neglected and repressed there flourished a vibrancy and dynamism in the Principality which, by the last decades of the century, had established, especially in South Wales, an industrial supremacy of world importance. Yet, despite the explosive growth of the Welsh economy in the south, much of Wales, especially in its more remote rural areas, was still cast in the mould of centuries, that 'feudalism' of social control and political dominance which Henry Richard found so abhorrent. Until 1868 Welsh politics was dominated by the gentry or, through their gentry connections, by the great aristocracy. And not only did the gentry dominate Welsh politics, they dominated the whole life of the countryside. Herbert Vaughan, writing in 1926, could say, with some nostalgia, that 'until some forty years ago the gentry . . . were the real rulers of the countryside. They interpreted the law at Petty Sessions; they were responsible for all local administration at Quarter Sessions; they constituted in fact a ruling caste'.[1]

It was a ruling caste whose ascendancy differed little from what it had been in the sixteenth century. In 1873, according to John Bateman,[2] over sixty per cent of Wales comprised estates of over a thousand acres controlled by only one per cent – some 571 families – of the totality of Welsh landowners. These families included the great dynasties, from the Butes and the Beauforts in the south to the Wynns, the Herberts and the Douglas-Pennants in the north. But beneath the great families lay a whole range of lesser squires and landlords throughout Wales, frequently bound together by marriage connection and social and economic interest. Nevertheless, despite their dominance of the political scene and of local administration and despite, in many instances, their concern for the welfare of their tenants and for the maintenance of harmonious relations with them, there had developed by the middle of the nineteenth century a divergence in social attitudes between landlords and their local communities that was to create estrangement and, at times, bitter conflict. English-speaking, Anglican in religion and, more often than not, Tory in politics, Welsh landlords were finding themselves confronted by a local community and a tenantry different in language and in religious and political convictions. A local community, too, energised and too easily impassioned by Nonconformist leaders who saw the solution of the inequalities of dissent being achieved only through the overthrow of the political ascendancy of the landlord classes.

The 'great election' of 1868, following the previous year's Reform Act and the expansion of the electorate, has been perceived as the beginning of the erosion of the landlords' political base. But it was the election of 1880 that was really to mark a shift in political authority in Wales. Twenty-nine of the thirty-three Welsh seats fell to the Liberals. And, as in Montgomeryshire, where the manufacturer Stuart Rendel defeated Charles Watkin Williams Wynn in the face of the combined forces of Wynnstay and Powis Castle, the majority of the new M.P.s were no longer landowners, but industrialists and manufacturers, or else barristers and solicitors.

The dominance of the landed interest over national politics in Wales had effectively come to an end, and, with the Local Government Act of 1888, its administrative power base in the localities was swept away: it was, in Vaughan's words 'a blow that in Wales smote the whole class beyond recovery'.[3] With the introduction of urban and district councils in 1894 the dominance of the landed gentry over local government in Wales finally ended, although this was not to say that the influence of individuals did not continue even to the present day. As the acknowledged *political* leaders of the community, however, the landed gentry gave way to more populist spokesmen and, such was the relationship between dissent and radicalism, that not infrequently it was Nonconformist ministers who came to the fore.

The decline of their political power did not, however, lessen radical antipathy to the gentry. In the 1880s the Welsh land question, highlighted by the agricultural depression of these years, in which, in fact, many landlords suffered more than their tenants, came very much to the fore. What was perceived, unfairly, as a general pattern of exploitation on the part of landlords was taken up quickly by radical politicians. Some allegations, like the evictions after the 1859 election on the Rhiwlas estate, had some foundation, but many were grossly exaggerated or had little substance. Myths, nevertheless, can be more potent than reality and in 1893 Gladstone set up a royal commission under the chairmanship of the radical Liberal Lord Carrington, that same Lord Carrington who had been involved with *Vanity Fair* in its early years. After an exhaustive hearing lasting two and a half years the Commission reported, but by then the land question had become less urgent. If the Commission had achieved anything, however, it had allowed the radical lobby to air its grievances and had exploded many of the allegations that had been made against the landowning community over the years.

Charles Watkin Williams Wynn by 'Spy', Vanity Fair *28 June 1879*.

Lord Carrington by 'Spy', Vanity Fair *11 September 1907*.

[1] Herbert M. Vaughan, *The Welsh Squires* (London 1926), p. 3.
[2] John Bateman, *The Great Landowners of Great Britain and Ireland* (London 1876).
[3] Vaughan, op. cit., p. 3.

SIR WATKIN WILLIAMS WYNN (1820-1885)

The King of Wales

Sir Watkin Williams Wynn, the sixth baronet, was head of one of the great landowning dynasties of Wales, controlling a domain of 148,000 acres from Wynnstay, near Wrexham. Rightly could he be described by *Vanity Fair* as 'the King of Wales', for with his land-ownership went immense political influence. After a traditional education and a short military career he turned his attention to the responsibilities of his estates and was noted as being one of the best landlords in North Wales who took pride in his relations with his tenants. In no way could he be castigated as 'cruel, unreasonable, unfeeling and unpitying', which were the labels so often pinned upon his fellow landlords by the radical lobby. The family had held the parliamentary seat for Denbighshire since the Jacobite uprising of 1715, and Sir Watkin succeeded to it in 1841. He held the seat for more than forty years, although 'Jehu Junior' alleged that this was 'without opening his mouth, otherwise than as a mark of the amount of interest he took in the debates'. In 1885 Sir Watkin died and in the great election later that year, under new constituency boundaries, with an enlarged electorate, and a by-now effective secret ballot, his son, the new Sir Watkin, succumbed to Liberal pressures and was defeated by the barrister Osborne Morgan. Even the largest landowner in the county, with 28,000 acres of land in the constituency, could not withstand the Liberal tide.

Already by 1880 the social and political ascendancy of the *plas* was fast disintegrating and a new bourgeoisie of industry and the law was replacing the traditional members in Parliament. Before the decade was out, too, the influence of the landowner in local government had been curtailed. Nevertheless, the beneficent landowner could still be held in esteem and 'Old Sir Watkin' was to be remembered for generations to come as a respected if paternalistic figure.

Vanity Fair: 14 June 1873. Leslie Ward.

EDWARD JAMES HERBERT, EARL OF POWIS (1818-1891)

Mouldy

The great-grandson of Clive of India, Edward James Herbert, succeeded to the Earldom of Powis in 1848 on the death of his father, who had earlier adopted his own mother's family name of Herbert.

A classical scholar of some distinction himself, Powis took an active interest in the cultural life of Wales and, as befitted the social position of an amateur scholar in his time, he was President of the Cambrian Archaeological Association in 1856 and of the Honourable Society of Cymmrodorion in 1885. Powis played an active role in the development of intermediate education in Montgomeryshire and was one of the promoters of the North Wales University College, being elected President of its Site and Organisation Committee in 1883. A year later, on its foundation, he became first President of the College, an office in which, the historian of the College tells us, 'he displayed ripe judgement and was always conscientious in attending to the minutest affairs'. A High Churchman, he was renowned for his generous help for church building and restoration but was always ready to support Nonconformist chapels in areas where there was no Anglican church. As a great landowner Powis had considerable influence in the Conservative interest, especially in eastern Montgomeryshire, but fair though he was recognised to be to his tenants, the family ascendency over local life could not prevent the unseating of Charles Williams Wynn by Stuart Rendel in 1880. This ascendancy effectively came to an end, in local politics, with Powis's rejection as Chairman of the new Montgomeryshire County Council in 1889.

Vanity Fair was perhaps less than fair to Powis. It took a jaundiced view of the family's renunciation of its original name, condemning the Clives for having 'disavowed the only great man of their race and elected to hang on to the remains of a more effete name [and] . . . since presented themselves for the ancient aristocracy of the country'. Lord Powis it described as 'a decent old gentleman of eight and fifty, eminent in mediocrity, and entitled to the respect which should surround a man who has not removed his neighbours' landmarks, and who is earnest in attendance at Quarter Sessions. Years ago he was a Member of Parliament by election, which would be surprising were it not that he was elected for a county subject to the family influence . . . He is a very decent person, and patronises sixteen livings'.

Vanity Fair: 27 May 1876. Leslie Ward.

RICHARD JOHN LLOYD PRICE (1843-1923)

Pointers

The Prices of Rhiwlas are of ancient Welsh ancestry, 'so old' suggested 'Jehu Junior', 'that the present head of the family is able to show a written pedigree tracing his descent back to the original Adam'.

R. J. Lloyd Price who succeeded to the Rhiwlas estates in 1860, devoted his life primarily to sporting pursuits. Price naturally undertook the local duties expected of a country landowner. He was an active magistrate and Deputy-Lieutenant for Merioneth and served as a Justice of the Peace in both Denbighshire and Caernarfonshire, into which counties the Price estates extended. A Conservative in politics 'he has hitherto', noted *Vanity Fair* 'steadfastly declined to stand for his county, alleging in refusal that "the company in the best club in England is not what it used to be"'. But he was the grandson of the R. W. Price, who, although an enlightened agriculturist, had been responsible for the Rhiwlas evictions following the election of 1859, and Price in turn was energetically supportive of the new Conservative candidate, W.R.M. Wynne of Peniarth, in 1865. Price's prime interests were sporting, however. One of the first changes that he made on coming into his inheritance was the introduction of game on the Rhiwlas estates and his *battues* and his hospitality on these occasions became proverbial. Price became especially notable as a breeder and judge of pointers and was the originator of 'Field Trials with the Gun'. He wrote a number of books on subjects as characteristic as *Rabbits for Profit and Rabbits for Powder*, *Practical Pheasant Rearing, with an Appendix on Grouse Driving* and *Dogs Ancient and Modern and Walks in Wales*. So fond was Price of his dogs that he created a small canine cemetery near Rhiwlas mansion. The success of his race-horse 'Bendigo' was even commemorated over the family vault in Llanfor churchyard:

> *I bless the good horse Bendigo*
> *That built this tomb for me.*

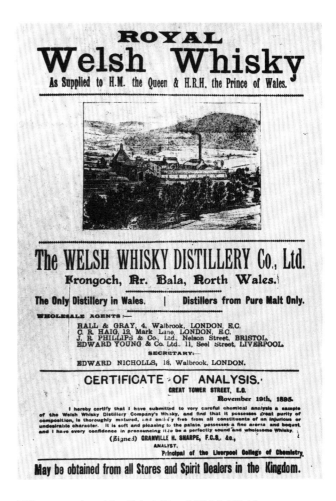

Bill-poster advertising Price's Royal Welsh Whisky.

Sport did not entirely dominate Price's life and he embarked upon a number of speculative industrial or commercial ventures, primarily it would seem, in an attempt to alleviate unemployment in a period of depression. A clay works, a slate quarry, a brush factory and, above all, the Welsh Whisky Distillery, all took their turn, but none proved successful. Not even the Distillery whose product was said to be 'the most wonderful whisky that ever drove the skeleton from the feast or painted landscapes in the brain of man'.

Vanity Fair: 10 October 1885. Leslie Ward.

SIR JOHN TALBOT DILLWYN LLEWELYN
(1836-1927)

Swansea

John Talbot Dillwyn Llewelyn was the grandson of Lewis Weston Dillwyn, proprietor of the famous Cambrian Pottery in Swansea and manufacturer of Swansea porcelain in the early nineteenth century. Retiring from his direct concern in the Pottery in 1817 – in which he had never been especially active – Lewis Weston Dillwyn had turned to public affairs and, from 1832 to 1837, he sat as a Whig member for Glamorgan in the Reform Parliament. At heart, though, Dillwyn's prime interest was in natural history and he achieved great distinction as a scientist, particularly in the fields of botany and conchology: he was elected a Fellow of the Royal Society in 1804 when only twenty-six.

In 1807 Dillwyn married the heiress of John Llewelyn of Penllergaer and Ynysgerwn, a marriage which not only brought him into county landowning circles but helped to make him one of the richest and most influential men in South Wales. When Dillwyn's eldest son, John, came of age in 1831 he inherited his maternal grandfather's considerable wealth and adopted his mother's family name to become known as John Dillwyn Llewelyn of Penllergaer. He inherited to the full his father's botanic interests and, in turn, was himself elected to the Royal Society in 1836. With Fox Talbot – a cousin through marriage – he made important improvements in photography and with Wheatstone he collaborated on the development of the electric telegraph. Through the consummate artistry of his photography and the dedication of his scientific endeavour Llewelyn bridged the divide between art and science. With his father, the Vivians, Grove, and others he helped to make Swansea the scientific and cultural centre it was in the second quarter of the nineteenth century.

John Dillwyn Llewelyn's son – the subject of 'Spy's' cartoon – again inherited his grandfather's love of botany and of entomology and acted as honorary curator in these subjects for the Royal Institution of South Wales. To the public at large he was, perhaps, best known for his development of the potato but John Talbot Dillwyn Llewelyn's prime concern was with the management of his estates and with his business interests as a director of the Great Western Railway. 'One of the principal landlords in South Wales', in Herbert Vaughan's words, Llewelyn owned some 15,000 acres. He was a staunch Conservative Unionist of great influence in the Swansea area, playing an active role in local public life and politics, for which he was rewarded with a baronetcy in 1880. A major figure locally, it was only after several unsuccessful attempts that he entered Parliament in 1895 by capturing Swansea Town from the Liberals in their heavy electoral defeat of that year and he remained an M.P. for only five years. Llewelyn took a particular interest in both secondary and higher education in Wales and was closely associated with St. David's College, Lampeter and the University College at Cardiff. He was one of the landowner members of the Royal Commission on Welsh Land (1893-1896) signing the minority report. Recognised as an efficient and tolerant landlord, Llewelyn was remembered with respect and affection long after his death at the age of ninety-one.

Vanity Fair: 11 October 1900. Leslie Ward.

The Political Scene

Vanity Fair spanned a period of profound change in British politics. The magazine saw the foundation of the modern political party system from the loose coalitions of the 1860s to the consolidated party machines of the twentieth century, the widening of the franchise and the gradual democratisation of the political structure with the eventual emergence of the Trade Unions and the Labour party as political forces. A period, too, in which the landed interest's grip on politics, both local and national, gradually lessened and in which a new kind of politician emerged into prominence from the commercial, professional and, in due course, the working classes.

When *Vanity Fair* first appeared in 1868 the political scene was still very much dominated by the landed gentry and nowhere was the landowning ascendancy more apparent than in Wales. During the middle years of the century, it is true, a yearning for political change had begun to be infused into the grass roots culture of the Principality. This was due in large part to the activities of the Liberation Society, which stood for the separation of Church and State, and, in the main, to the unwearied campaigning of Henry Richard on its behalf. Through the creation of 'Liberationist' branches in Wales a political dimension was added to the grievances of Nonconformity over the inequalities of dissent in the face of the dominance of the established Church.

Edward Miall, campaigner for the disestablishment of the Church and founder of the Liberation Society, by 'Ape', Vanity Fair *29 July 1871.*

Miall greatly influenced the Liberationist campaign in Wales. A master of bitter invective, like many of the dissenting leaders, he saw the established Church as 'a stupendous money scheme carried on under false pretences – a bundle of vested rights, stamped for greater security with the sacred name of Christianity'.

It was not, however, until the extension of the franchise by Disraeli in 1867 that the pressures created by 'Liberationists' bore some fruit. In the so-called 'great election' of 1868 something of a new face was given to Welsh politics, not that any change of moment occurred in the social grouping of those elected: although twenty-three of the new Welsh Members were Liberal as opposed to ten Conservatives, the bulk of the Liberals were still landowners and of Whiggish persuasion. Nevertheless, three of the new Members – including Richard himself – were Nonconformists and Welsh Nonconformity now had a voice in the House, a voice that was to become increasingly strident as the years went by. What was to be of significance, too, was the aftermath of the 1868 election and the evictions of tenants in Carmarthenshire and Cardiganshire who had not followed the traditional lead of the local gentry. Whether or not, as A. H. Dodd suggests, this implied 'a waning self-confidence among the country's historic leaders', the evictions, skilfully and passionately cultivated by Richard, led not only to the Ballot Act of 1872 but, in Wales, helped to re-inforce the political polarisation of Anglican, English-speaking gentry on the one hand and Nonconformist, Welsh-speaking tenantry on the other.

The 'great election' otherwise had little immediate political effect. Not for another decade was any collective approach to Welsh issues, such as disestablishment, to be developed. For the time being the Welsh Members were left individually to devote their energies to problems that interested them personally, such as burial rights, education and the cause of international peace. Even Richard, 'the Member for Wales', exerted little cohesive influence at this time.

More lasting change came with the general election of 1886 which was fought against a background of an enlarged electorate and new constituency boundaries. The old political order was now seen to be coming to an end. The Liberals won thirty of the thirty-four Welsh seats and, with the establishment of the Liberal ascendancy, the impact of the Welsh dimension began to be felt at Westminster and was to continue until the Great War.

With the introduction of a new breed of Welsh Member – radical, Nonconformist and middle-class professional – a new flavour was introduced into British politics. This new generation of Welsh Liberals – Tom Ellis, Samuel Evans, D. A. Thomas and David Lloyd George – was more aggressive, politically sophisticated and nationalistic than the more traditional Welsh Liberals as typified by men such as Osborne Morgan and even Lewis Llewelyn Dillwyn and Henry Richard. They formed a new, powerful and effective pressure group and through the formation of the Welsh Parliamentary Party had the means to ensure recognition of their demands for Wales.

Although Welsh nationalism was a unifying cause, the demands for separatism and independence through home rule tended to be muted. Practical issues such as land tenure, temperance, the educational system and the disestablishment of the Church dominated the political agenda, and, through Parliamentary debate, more was achieved in real terms for Wales in these years than for Ireland through the bitter conflict generated by the Irish revolt.

Parliament reached its apogee in later Victorian times and politicians were a natural target for the caricaturists of *Vanity Fair*. Their activities provided an endless stream of material for the accompanying satirical commentaries. In all, over a third of the portraits in the magazine were of politicians, from private Members to ministers of the Crown. With the exception of Palmerston and Aberdeen every Prime Minister from Lord John Russell (1846-1852) to Andrew Bonar Law (1922-1923) was represented in *Vanity Fair*.

Earl Russell (Lord John Russell), Prime Minister 1846-1852 and 1865-1866, by 'Ape', Vanity Fair 5 June 1869. Vanity Fair *described Russell as 'the greatest Liberal statesman of modern times'. Russell was short in stature and spoke with a small, thin voice.*

The caricatures and the biographical sketches that went with them present a rich historical survey of political life in the late Victorian and Edwardian period and also provide a remarkable insight into one of the most formative periods of political history, which brought significant change to British society and laid the foundations of the modern state.

SIR EDWARD JAMES REED (1830-1906)

Naval Construction

From lowly beginnings as an apprentice shipwright through a brilliant, if somewhat stormy, career as a warship designer Edward James Reed rose to become the Chief Constructor of the Navy. His designs revolutionised the construction of warships but finding himself in dispute with the Admiralty over alterations to his seminal plans for H.M.S. *Devastation* and in the wake of the loss of H.M.S. *Captain*, whose design he had opposed, Reed resigned to join Sir Joseph Whitworth in 1870. Establishing a successful private practice Reed designed warships for several foreign navies, including those of Japan and Germany, as well as receiving commissions from his former employers, the Admiralty.

Of great influence in his profession Reed was the first secretary of the Institute of Naval Architects and, as the Navy's Chief Constructor, was instrumental in establishing the Royal School of Naval Architecture and Marine Engineering in 1864.

At the time of the *Captain* controversy Reed had apparently talked of entering Parliament and in 1874 he was elected for Pembroke Boroughs as a Liberal, with a majority of twenty-nine. Six years later he transferred to Cardiff – the largest single-member constituency in the Kingdom, as Reed was prone to point out – which he represented in the Liberal interest until 1895 and again from 1900 until 1905 when he retired. Prickly, pugnacious and very much a stormy petrel, Reed was described by Stuart Rendel as a 'self-seeking bully and impostor'. As a Welsh Liberal M.P. his attitude to the great issues of the day, temperance, home rule and disestablishment, was often ambivalent and he was suspected as being 'probably out of sympathy with the national aspirations of the Welsh people'. To Rendel, his interest seemed almost wholly confined to dockyards (Milford Haven docks are his monument). Brusque and hot tempered as he was Reed was an excellent constituency M.P. and commanded a strong personal following in his sprawling and heterogeneous electoral division, where any common attitude to the Welsh issues of the day was unlikely to be obvious.

In 1902 he was accused of being one of those Liberals 'who long since should have taken an excursion ticket to Toryism which was his proper station'. This he did in 1904 and resigned his seat over the tariff question.

Vanity Fair: 20 March 1875. Carlo Pellegrini.

HENRY CECIL RAIKES (1839-1891)

The son of a Welsh barrister from Flint, Henry Cecil Raikes was educated at Shrewsbury and Cambridge. Called to the Bar in 1863 his practical interest in the law soon became secondary to his interest in politics and in 1868 he entered Parliament as Conservative M.P. for Chester. Although still only thirty-five the reputation he made in his first years in the Commons secured his election as Chairman of the Committee of Ways and Means and Deputy Speaker in 1874, when the Conservatives came to power under Disraeli. Raikes soon found himself confronted with the unenviable task of coping with the obstructionist tactics of the Parnellites.

Losing his seat in the election of 1880 he returned to the House as M.P. for Preston in 1882, resigning that, in turn, to become the Member for Cambridge University. Government office came to him eventually with his appointment as Postmaster General in 1886. Although not a great innovator, during his tenure of office he established the first telephonic link with Paris in 1891 and introduced the express messenger service.

Not a great speaker Raikes did have the reputation of being a skilful debater – he had been President of the Cambridge Union – but in the heated debates on Welsh issues in the 1880s he could be abusive and denigratory: he once described Welsh nationality as being of interest only to students of folk-lore and archaeology. He was an ardent defender of the Church in the tithe and disestablishment debates of those years and in 1890 became Chancellor of his home diocese of St. Asaph.

To 'Jehu Junior' he had no weaknesses apart from being Chairman of the Church Defence Institution and having 'a taste for writing poetry, which is only redeemed by the fact that he never publishes it': some was, in fact, posthumously published in 1896.

Vanity Fair: 17 April 1875. Carlo Pellegrini.

SIR GEORGE OSBORNE MORGAN (1826-1897)

Burials

The eldest son of Morgan Morgan, the Vicar of Conwy, George Osborne Morgan was educated at Shrewsbury – where his headmaster, the redoubtable Benjamin Hall Kennedy, said of him that he had never known a boy 'with such a vast amount of undigested information' – and Oxford, where he had a brilliant undergraduate career before becoming a Fellow of University College. He soon decided against an academic career, however, and became a Chancery lawyer. Turning to politics while still active in chambers Morgan became a close associate of Edward Miall, the leader of the Nonconformist political radicals, and took up the causes of church disestablishment and the abolition of religious tests in the universities.

In 1868, on the recommendation of Edward Miall and Thomas Gee, Morgan was adopted as a Liberal candidate for Denbighshire, a seat he held until the redistribution of constituencies in 1885, when he wrested East Denbighshire from the Wynn family and brought to an end their 182-year representation of the county. In Parliament he took a prominent part in Welsh affairs; in 1869 he seconded Henry Richard's resolution on the Welsh evictions after the election of 1868, and in 1870 he introduced his first burials bill to allow any Christian service in a parish churchyard. Morgan introduced this bill in ten successive sessions until, in 1880, it was eventually passed. He was a strong supporter of the Welsh Sunday Closing Bill and, naturally, throughout his parliamentary career, of disestablishment. Under Gladstone he twice achieved junior ministerial office. In 1880 he was appointed Judge-Advocate-General and introduced the Army Discipline Bill which abolished flogging, and six years later was appointed Parliamentary Under Secretary for the Colonies. Although only holding office for six months he succeeded in establishing the Emigration Inquiry Office in response to the problems encountered by Welsh settlers in Patagonia.

Morgan's overriding interest, however, was education. He played an active part in the foundation of the University Colleges of Aberystwyth and Bangor, and, as a supporter of education for women, was involved in the establishment of a women's hostel at Bangor. Although by no means a fluent Welsh speaker he served as Vice-President of the National Eisteddfod Association, and, in addition, was prominent in the affairs of the Honourable Society of Cymmrodorion.

Morgan was made a baronet in 1892. 'Jehu Junior' saw him as 'a quiet but pleasant man, very industrious, very earnest, and with a considerable future before him'. To the waspish T. Marchant Williams, Morgan's career evinced 'a curious recurrence of failures . . . Were Mr. Gladstone asked his opinion of Sir George he would probably say of him, with the late Master of Balliol, "Osborne Morgan is a very clever fellow, but –"'. Certainly, the future charted by 'Jehu Junior' was a future that Morgan never quite fulfilled.

Vanity Fair: 17 May 1879. Leslie Ward.

HENRY RICHARD (1812-1888)

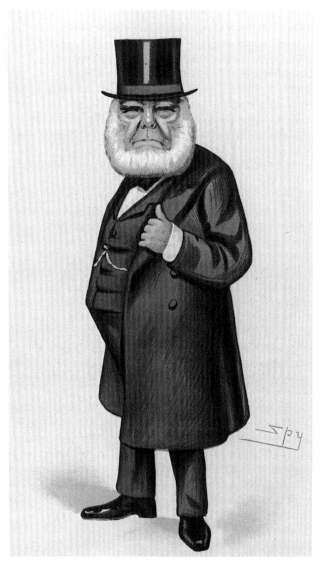

Peace

The son of a Calvinist minister, Henry Richard was born in Tregaron. In 1826, after Llangeitho Grammar School, he was apprenticed to a Carmarthen draper. Later, he studied at Highbury College and in 1835 he was ordained as minister of Marlborough Congregational Chapel in the Old Kent Road, where he remained until his retirement from the ministry in 1850.

An ardent pacifist, Richard was often called the 'Apostle of Peace'. He became Secretary of the Peace Society in 1848 and was influential in organising a number of international peace conferences over the succeeding decade. The advocacy of arbitration as a means of settling international disputes was very much Richard's life's work. To 'Jehu Junior' his approach was naive. 'Regarding the Powers of Europe as being in the main good little children he [Richard] appears honestly to believe it possible that when the intention is formed to do unlawful acts and the strength to do them is felt, the intention can be changed otherwise than by armed resistence. This belief is the measure of Mr. Richard's political capacity and the motive of most of his public acts . . . He desires Peace at any price except at the price of taking the only methods of resisting lawlessness which can ensure it'. Despite *Vanity Fair*'s cynicism Richard was instrumental in securing an arbitration clause in the Treaty of Paris that ended the Crimean War.

A leading member of the Liberation Society and an advanced Liberal, Richard gave notable service to Wales. An effective critic of the 'Blue Books' in 1847 he sought, through the years, to interpret Wales to the English and his series of letters upon the social and political condition of the Principality, coupled with his other public utterances, unfair, exaggerated and polemical as they often were, attracted wide attention.

In 1862, Richard was, with Edward Miall and other prominent members of the Liberation Society, present at a great Nonconformist gathering in Swansea to commemorate those who had suffered under the Clarendon Code. This conference, well orchestrated, marked the beginnings of an effective organisation in Wales in which dissent and advanced Liberalism could be combined to achieve both disestablishment and the removal of those disabilities, political and social, to which Welsh Nonconformists were subject.

His political career already well advanced, and with a reputation as a Nonconformist publicist long established, Richard was returned as Member of Parliament for Merthyr, (defeating Henry Austin Bruce) in the celebrated election of the *Annus Mirabilis* of 1868. From the first Richard was regarded as 'the member for Wales'. He took a leading part in Parliament in exposing the tenantry evictions following the 1868 election and although by now reluctantly reconciled to the principle of state aid in education he was tireless in opposing those clauses of the 1870 Education Bill which he considered obnoxious to Nonconformists. A firm upholder of Welsh and Nonconformist rights he was very much to the fore in the debates both in and out of Parliament on disestablishment and burial rights.

Closely associated with the Aberystwyth College, his strong interest in education in Wales led to his appointment in 1880 to the Departmental Committee on Intermediate and Higher Education in Wales under Lord Aberdare that led to the establishment of the Welsh University Colleges and eventually, through the Intermediate Education Act of 1889, to the creation of a secondary education system in Wales.

Passionate and pugnacious as he was, Richard was a man of deep religious convictions, who worked unstintingly throughout his life for what he saw as the true interests of peace, Wales and dissent. The belligerent, uncompromising character of the 'Apostle of Peace' is well brought out in 'Spy's' cartoon.

Vanity Fair: 4 September 1880. Leslie Ward.

LEWIS LLEWELYN DILLWYN (1814-1892)

A Wet Quaker

Lewis Llewelyn Dillwyn, the second son of Lewis Weston Dillwyn, inherited his father's scholarly interests and was an amateur scientist of no mean attainment. He married the daughter of the geologist Sir Henry de la Beche. When his father became one of the two Members for Glamorgan in the Reform Parliament of 1832, more out of a sense of duty than of inclination, Lewis Dillwyn began to take over management of the Cambrian Pottery. However, lacking his father's firmness and business acumen, it was a venture in which Dillwyn was never particularly successful. Indeed, none of his industrial and commercial involvements was successful in financial terms and when he died in 1892 his affairs were in dire straits.

Nevertheless, whatever his own personal financial difficulties, perhaps due more to bad advice than his own incompetence, Lewis Dillwyn played a prominent role in the industrial development of Swansea. He was head of the Landore Spelter Works and was closely associated with Siemens in the Landore-Siemens Steel Company of which he was Chairman. The Glamorganshire Banking Company and the Great Western Railway were also prime interests.

Dillwyn's real concern, however, was politics. In 1855 he succeeded John Henry Vivian as Member of Parliament for Swansea and served as an M.P. until his death in 1892, from 1885 as Member for the newly-formed Swansea Town division. Although Lewis Dillwyn had been instrumental with his elder brother in putting down the 'Rebecca' raid on the Pontarddulais toll gate in 1843 he had acknowledged the basic justice of the rioters' cause and, in politics, inherited to the full his father's liberal outlook. Indeed, in Parliament he became a pronounced radical. He championed the cause of the Cardiganshire farmers evicted for their votes in the 1868 election and of the Denbighshire tenantry who, in 1886-1887, agitated against tithes. He was from the earliest days a prominent member of the Liberation Society and in Parliament the greatest champion of disestablishment of the Welsh Church, which he so often alleged had 'failed to fulfil its objects'. From 1883 Dillwyn was himself the proposer of almost annual resolutions in support of disestablishment. He later became a supporter of Irish Home Rule. Although something of an eccentric – he thought nothing of walking the four miles home from the station after an arduous day in London – and celebrated as an advanced Liberal, he none-the-less remained throughout his life a man of considerable standing both in Glamorgan county society and in the somewhat different urban society of Swansea. To 'Jehu Junior' Dillwyn was 'in private life . . . a most amiable person; in public life he is a great partisan, and believes himself to be an authority on order, which he is always infringing. He speaks very badly; he is rather dull; he is a great admirer of Mr. Gladstone; he votes in every Radical division . . . and is altogether a most uncompromising partisan. Yet he is a good and kindly man, and there is no real harm in him'. Originally Quakers the Dillwyns, since Lewis Weston's time, had become Anglicans. Thus lapsed from Friendship they had become 'Wet Quakers'.

Vanity Fair: 13 May 1882. Leslie Ward.

HON FREDERIC COURTENAY MORGAN
(1834-1909)

Fred

The third son of the first Lord Tredegar, Frederic Morgan, like his next elder brother Godfrey, who took part in the Charge of the Light Brigade at Balaclava, served in the Crimean War with distinction.

In 1874 Morgan became M.P. for the family seat, Monmouthshire – held, with few breaks, by the Morgans since 1547 – for which he sat until the redistribution of seats following the Reform Act of 1884. Thereafter he represented the southern division of the county, unruffled by Liberal opposition, until the great landslide of 1906, when he was finally unseated together with all five of the other Welsh Conservatives. Morgan was typical of the old school of Welsh county Member. 'Jehu Junior' described him as 'a wholesome Tory who respects the integrity of the Empire'. It was an exaggeration to accuse him of 'never [having] been found guilty of making a speech in the House'. He certainly did speak against disestablishment, but in 1905 D. A. Thomas estimated that Fred Morgan's speeches over his time in Parliament had amounted to five seconds a year. Nonetheless, he remained in the judgement of *Vanity Fair* 'a very popular fellow . . . [who] . . . wears a very beautiful moustache which but half conceals a genial smile'.

Vanity Fair: 2 November 1893. Leslie Ward.

JAMES KEIR HARDIE (1856-1915)

Queer Hardie

Born in a one-roomed cottage in Lanarkshire, Keir Hardie, an illegitimate child, was brought up in extreme poverty. At seven he became a messenger boy, then he worked for a time in a ship-yard, and afterwards as a baker's errand boy. From the age of ten until he was twenty-three he worked in the Lanarkshire coalmines. During this time he attended evening school, and, a severe evangelical, he became an active worker in the temperance movement. This was his introduction to politics and by the later 1870s he had begun to agitate for better conditions among the mineworkers, then very badly paid and virtually unorganised, but his activities cost him and his two younger brothers their jobs.

In 1878 Hardie started a stationery business and took up journalism for a local newspaper. He decided now, too, to try in earnest to organise the mineworkers and for many years he acted as the unpaid official of a number of miners' associations. In 1886 he became secretary of the Scottish miners' federation, formed by the various county unions which he had helped to create but paid little or nothing for his services, he supported himself mainly by journalism. At this time he still regarded himself as a Liberal but, assailed by increasing doubts about the party's capability to act as a true instrument for working-class reform, by 1887 he had begun to promote the idea of a distinct Labour party. In 1892 he was elected as independent Labour Member of Parliament for West Ham South, the election in which John Burns was returned for Battersea. Hardie's election undoubtedly helped forward the movement for an independent working-class party, and early in 1893 the Independent Labour Party was formed, with Hardie as chairman. In Parliament Hardie rapidly made his name as 'the member for the unemployed', adopting from the first a militant stance on this issue. In 1895 he lost his seat owing to the withdrawal of support by the Liberals but in 1900, after some unsuccessful attempts to return to Parliament, he was elected for Merthyr in the 'Khaki' election as running-mate to D. A. Thomas, the Liberal coalowner. This seat he held continuously until his death.

Hardie took an active part in forming the Labour Representation Committee in 1900. When this became the Labour Party, and a strong Labour group was for the first time returned to Parliament in 1906, Hardie became its first leader in the House of Commons; but he resigned the leadership, owing to illness, in the following year. In 1913 he again became chairman of the Independent Labour Party, a position which he had held from 1893 to 1900.

Hardie was, in his day, perhaps the best-hated and the best-loved man in Great Britain. Passionate in his language he was uncompromising to his opponents and was commonly regarded as much more of an extremist than he really was. In the Labour movement, on the other hand, he was viewed with feelings almost of veneration, and his personal popularity was immense. Acutely class-conscious and proud, to a degree, of his origins and attitude, he wore the cloth cap and tweed suit, which so scandalised Parliament when he first took his seat in 1892, partly at least, as a dramatic gesture to help him sustain this character. 'Spy's' portrait, perhaps surprisingly, paints an affectionate picture of Hardie. Here we have, in tweeds and with pipe, no archetypal revolutionary but a man of solid good sense, a man, whom 'Jehu Junior' could say was 'worthy of attention'.

Vanity Fair: 8 February 1906. Leslie Ward.

DAVID LLOYD GEORGE, EARL LLOYD GEORGE (1863-1945)

A Nonconformist Genius

Lloyd George has been seen as one of the most inspired and creative statesmen of the twentieth century. To others he has appeared opportunistic and devious, a politician whose character and career were far from being praiseworthy. No British political leader has attracted so much esteem or generated such opprobrium. But whatever one's view of this controversial figure no-one can doubt Lloyd George's dominance of the British political scene in the first quarter of the twentieth century. He was the architect of the modern welfare state and the vital leader of the nation in the Great War. For all his failings – and they were many – in A. J. P. Taylor's words 'it is difficult to resist the feeling that he was the greatest ruler of Britain since Oliver Cromwell'.

The son of a schoolmaster from Pembrokeshire, Lloyd George was born in Manchester but, when only eighteen months old, his father died and he was taken to live with his uncle, a shoemaker, in Llanystumdwy, a village near Cricieth in Caernarfonshire. From the local village school he entered a solicitor's office in Cricieth, eventually setting up his own practice in the town. Stirred by the radical passions agitating rural Wales and imbibing the democratic dissenting values of his uncle, Lloyd George soon became involved in local politics. His legal practice was a powerful political base and through his handling of the defence in the Llanfrothen burial case in 1888 his name became a household word throughout Non-conformist Wales. In 1890 he was elected Liberal Member for Caernarfon Boroughs at the age of twenty-seven. From the

very beginning, with a maiden speech on temperance, Lloyd George frequently made his presence felt in the House, although a fellow Liberal dismissed his early utterances as 'incoherent declamations'. Nevertheless, he soon earned a reputation as a speaker of some eloquence. Until 1896 he devoted himself to championing Welsh causes. Taken to task by colleagues 'as less of a Liberal than a Welshman on the loose', he limited his horizons to those questions that were uppermost in the mind of Welsh radical dissent: temperance, tithes, disestablishment and land reform. Encouraged by the progress of Irish home rule, he gradually convinced himself that the only way these issues could be resolved was by a large measure of independence from Whitehall. However, the collapse of his Welsh National League in 1896 made him rethink his position and brought Lloyd George much more into line with orthodox Liberal Party politics. From now on he rejected separatism and sought to link his concern for Welsh causes with broader British issues. The narrow nationalist politician had taken the path to imperial statesman. Because he was increasingly active in wider Parliamentary questions such as education and foreign affairs, his political career was almost ended by his bitter opposition to the Boer War, although, by 1902, the anti-war mood having now gripped the Liberal Party, Lloyd George became acceptable again to his main stream colleagues. In fact, as *Vanity Fair* was to point out, 'the war made Mr. Lloyd George'. It went on, though, to stress that 'even at the end of the war . . . no one dreamed of his constructive ability and fairmindedness'.

His first government appointment came in 1905 when he entered Campbell-Bannerman's cabinet as President of the Board of Trade. Here he was intimately involved over the debate on free trade and tariff reform and came into close contact with the world of business and commerce and with the trade unions. Indeed, his flair as a skilful negotiator came to the fore during this period as he successfully grappled with the settlement of a number of complex industrial disputes.

With the appointment of Asquith as Prime Minister in 1908, Lloyd George became Chancellor of the Exchequer. His 'People's Budget' of 1909 declared war on poverty and his tax reforms made future provision for social services. This revolutionary budget was rejected by the House of Lords and the ensuing constitutional crisis led to the General Election of 1910. Asquith's government was returned and Lloyd George continued as Chancellor with a remit to pursue further social reforms. In 1911 he launched his national insurance scheme and went on to initiate further social reforms in the fields of health, education, wages and employment. He was by now a national celebrity, but his plans for reform were curtailed by the outbreak of the Great War, and by November 1914 he was preparing his first war budget. Although still Chancellor of the Exchequer Lloyd George was drawn increasingly into the conduct of military strategy and was soon involved in conflict over policy and what he saw as Asquith's dilatory direction of the war.

With the formation of the coalition government in 1915, Lloyd George was put in charge of the newly-formed Ministry of Munitions. His Herculean efforts to organise industry to meet military needs turned the industrial system into a war economy under the centralist direction of his ministry and was a major contribution towards the war effort. In 1916, following the death of Kitchener – a particular *bête noire* of Lloyd George – he was appointed Secretary of State for War. At this time the war was going badly and Lloyd George became increasingly impatient with his inability to influence the army chiefs and the Cabinet. He talked of resigning, but following a political crisis late in 1916 that arose out of the military reverses of that year, Lloyd George found himself, with Conservative support, as Prime Minister.

As Prime Minister Lloyd George made himself into a virtual dictator for the duration of the war – 'the Big Beast of the Forest' – who, through his small War Cabinet and private team of advisers, exercised a supreme political leadership over both the home and war fronts. For all his faults he was the indispensable leader the nation needed. By 1918, he was at the peak of his career. He was 'the man who won the war' and 'the man who got things done'. But his triumph was at a heavy cost. He had split the Liberal Party and he headed a coalition government in which the Conservatives were dominant: he was wholly dependent upon them for survival.

In the aftermath of the war he led the world with Clemenceau and Wilson and became intimately committed to the search for an international settlement and to the efforts to promote the economic revival of Europe. At home, he had to see Britain through the transition from war to peace. But although he achieved a great deal he had to face the increasingly desperate situation in Ireland and the serious industrial difficulties that were arising from post-war social and economic problems. By 1922 Lloyd George's popular appeal had turned sour and his promises of a better post-war Britain – 'a land fit for heroes' – were seen as a cruel mockery: the nation was in the midst of what was described as 'one of the worst years of depression

since the industrial revolution'. Lloyd George's ruthless retaliation to the rebellion in Ireland had dismayed the Liberals and the Civil War which had now followed the settlement had disenchanted the Conservatives. His increasingly 'presidential' style of premiership both estranged and disillusioned his colleagues in government. Ever the opportunist, he sought to re-establish his dominance over his coalition through British involvement in a military conflict between Greece and Turkey. But even 'the wizard of Wales' for once misjudged the reaction at home: the British people felt they were being rushed into an unnecessary war and the more politically sensitive Conservatives broke the Coalition.

Lloyd George was never to hold high office again. Although the Liberals re-united as a party in 1923 and Lloyd George succeeded Asquith as their leader three years later, as a political force the party was spent, trailing Labour and very much in decline. Thus, while Lloyd George personally remained an important political figure for some time, his influence, such as it was, came to be more on the international stage and more in terms of ideas and policies than of practical politics.

'Spy's' cartoon captured both Lloyd George's dynamism and puckish charm, from the aggressive stance to the expressive hands and the irrepressible humour of the eyes. 'Jehu Junior' saw in Lloyd George the possibility of his reaching 'the highest office in the state: in our opinion there have been few Prime Ministers qualified to do great work for the country'. And this was in 1907 *before* he had become Chancellor.

Vanity Fair: 13 November 1907. Leslie Ward.

The Law

Since Tudor times Welshmen had been attracted to the law and the 'Welsh attorney', loquacious and devious by turn, was a figure not unknown to English literature. For many an ambitious and resourceful young man the law could offer not only a profitable career but also an *entrée* into politics. Indeed, for the eloquent Welshman a ready platform for his talents beckoned from court, hustings and Parliament. And as the dominance of the landed interest over Parliament was eroded it was industrialists and manufacturers, and especially barristers and solicitors, who came to the fore as Members of the Commons. In Wales, men like George Osborne Morgan, Henry Cecil Raikes, Samuel Evans and, above all, 'the little Welsh attorney' himself, Lloyd George, all made a considerable mark in politics in their time. But, of course, the vast majority of Welsh lawyers never forsook their profession, or, like Samuel Evans, returned to it, and some, like Evans again, rose to high office and became of sufficient stature to attract the attention of the *Vanity Fair* caricaturists.

The Bar and the Bench in particular, with the personal idiosyncrasies that the drama of the courts encouraged, provided the cartoonists with a rich source of material. The English judicial system itself, although considerably reformed during the last decades of the nineteenth century, was still not beyond criticism, and 'Jehu Junior' was swift to point out its shortcomings. And although members of the judiciary were seen to be incorruptible, they were prime targets for the caricaturist, their human foibles never escaping the satirist's pen. The advocates were an even more legitimate target and the magazine had no scruples when it came to criticising their advocatorial weaknesses, human frailties and rich, and often opulent, lifestyle.

The *Vanity Fair* caricatures of nineteenth century judges and barristers are, perhaps, today among the best-known and most cherished of the magazine's cartoons.

JOHN HUMFFREYS PARRY (1816-1880)

A Lawyer

John Humffreys Parry was the son of the Welsh antiquary and lawyer of the same name who had taken an active part in the revival of the Cymmrodorion Society in 1820. His father's murder in a tavern brawl dictated a commercial education for the young Parry, but after a short spell in a merchant's office in London he joined the printed books department of the British Museum. While there he attended lectures at the Aldersgate Institution and studied law. He was called to the Bar in 1843 and joined the home circuit where he soon developed a good criminal practice. Parry's appointment as one of the last serjeants-at-law, in 1856, assisted him, so his biographer tells us, 'to better work in the civil courts, where, thanks to an admirable appearance and voice, great clearness and simplicity of statement, and the tact of a born advocate, he was very successful in winning verdicts'. His best-known cases were the Overend and Gurney banking prosecution in 1869; the indictment of Arthur Orton, the Tichborne claimant, in 1873-4; and the libel action Whistler brought against Ruskin in 1878 for the latter's accusation that Whistler had flung 'a pot of paint in the public's face'.

In politics Parry was an advanced Liberal. At the time of the first Chartist movement he sympathised with the more moderate of their views, and knew many of their leaders, including William Lovett. Parry was also one of the founders of the Complete Suffrage Association in 1842. He was, however, never successful in winning a Parliamentary seat.

To *Vanity Fair* Parry's 'oratory . . . was – and still is – rather of the stumping kind; he is a believer in action so far as to impart it even to his wig by the action of his forehead; he drapes himself in his gown with the movement of a senator of melodrama, and his perorations have a boldness of flight which a confirmed ranter might envy'.

Parry died at his house in Kensington, of congestion of the lungs, aggravated, it is said, by the faulty drainage of the house.

Socially, and especially in his own profession, Serjeant Parry was highly regarded not only for the forensic talents, which made him for many years one of the best-known figures in the courts, but also for his kindliness and geniality which won him a very large circle of friends.

Vanity Fair: 13 December 1873. Leslie Ward.

SIR ROLAND BOWDLER VAUGHAN WILLIAMS (1838-1916)

The Mandarin

The descendant of a Welsh family long connected with the law, Roland Bowdler Vaughan Williams inherited and continued its tradition of fine scholarship and of distinction in that profession. His grandfather, Sergeant John Williams (1757-1810), had been a successful barrister from Carmarthen and his father, Sir Edward Vaughan Williams (1797-1875), was a Justice of the Court of Common Pleas from 1846 to 1865.

After graduating in jurisprudence and modern history at Christ Church, Oxford, Roland Vaughan Williams was called to the Bar in 1864. Establishing a successful common law practice over the next twenty-five years he earned a reputation for learning rather than advocacy. Indeed, his work *The Law and Practice of Bankruptcy*, published in 1870, was still the definitive text over half a century later.

His elevation to the judiciary came in 1890 with his appointment to the Queen's Bench Division, and his wide experience in the field of bankruptcy was put to good use when, in 1891, he was assigned to the bankruptcy jurisdiction of the High Court. His most important case came in 1894 when he presided over the liquidation of the New Zealand Loan and Mercantile Agency – a *cause célèbre* with major political implications as the then President of the Board of Trade, Anthony Mundella, was a director of the company.

Vaughan Williams's career reached its peak in 1897 with his appointment as a Lord Justice of Appeal, a judicial office he was to hold until his retirement seventeen years later. Every problem that confronted him was examined with thoroughness and if he was sometimes accused of possessing an over-subtle mind his courtesy to cousel helped to make him one of the most popular judges of his time. In his personal

appearance, his biographer tells us, he 'looked a strikingly picturesque survival from a bygone age'. Jehu Junior describes Vaughan Williams as 'for twenty years one of the familiar objects of the Temple, within whose precincts there was no shabbier man to look at save one; which one was his clerk . . . But since he has risen in the world he has bought a new great-coat . . . nor is he any longer to be seen munching an apple in the street in the morning nor carrying home a number of brown paper parcels in the evening'.

A Rustic Judge.

In 1906 Vaughan Williams was appointed Chairman of the Royal Commission into the Welsh Church question by the Campbell-Bannerman government. The Commission was viewed with great suspicion as a delaying measure by the government and Vaughan Williams's querulous attitude and rigid interpretation of his terms of reference served to make a contentious issue only more unlikely of solution. His thoroughness of examination, however, was brought out in the Commission's report when it was eventually published four years later. The report's detailed statistical evidence showed a Nonconformist preponderance in Wales of almost three to one which served to substantiate the claims of the spokesmen for disestablishment and, to an extent, contributed to the solution of the problem in due course.

Vanity Fair: 13 December 1890. John Page Mellor.
Vanity Fair: 2 March 1899. CGD.

SIR FREDERICK ALBERT BOSANQUET (1837-1923)

Bosey

Frederick Albert Bosanquet, a Bosanquet of Dingestow Court, Monmouthshire, came of an old Huguenot family. Educated at Eton and Cambridge, he was a Classical First, a Senior Optime and a Fellow of King's College. Called to the Bar in 1863 Bosanquet was for some years junior counsel to the Admiralty. In 1882 he took Silk and acquired a large practice both in London and on circuit, often appearing in local government cases. His arguments, full and learned though they were, were not always lively. But he was, in fact, a man of great humour and his after-dinner speeches were, reputedly, listened to with delight.

As a lawyer Bosanquet's reputation stood high and his appointment to the bench was always regarded as likely, but a High Court judgeship was never offered to him. In 1900, however, Bosanquet was chosen by Lord Halsbury as Common Serjeant of London. As Common Serjeant he had both criminal and civil jurisdiction – like a circuit judge today which the Common Sergent now is – and was equally at home at the Old Bailey or in the Mayor's Court.

According to 'Jehu Junior' Bosanquet 'once stood for Parliament, but the Election was over before he had time to state his case to the Electors'; yet as a barrister he was always in great demand as an arbitrator. He was, indeed, an admirable lawyer, if rather too slow and solemn to be a very successful advocate in any but the most ponderous cases. On circuit his portentous solemnity of manner earned him a reputation for wit; but another member of it once said (perhaps in jealousy) that the Oxford Circuit could not recognise wit when they met with it. Now he is quite a good Judge in the Mayor's Court and at the Old Bailey; for he is one of those men who do better as a Judge than as an advocate'.

Vanity Fair: 21 November 1901. Leslie Ward.

SIR SAMUEL THOMAS EVANS (1859-1918)

Samuel Evans was born in Skewen where his parents kept a grocer's shop. Educated initially at the Swansea Collegiate School, he was one of the early students of the newly founded Aberystwyth College where he took the London degree of LL.B. To Jehu Junior Evans could be said 'truly to be the brightest first-fruit of the modern educational movement in Wales'. His parents wanted him to enter the ministry but Evans, instead, qualified as a solicitor and for some time practised in Neath where he also became prominent in local politics. As a young 'Welsh home ruler' Evans entered Parliament in 1890 as member for Mid-Glamorgan, a seat which he was to hold continuously for the next twenty years. In 1891 Evans was called to the Bar and soon became one of the busiest juniors on the South Wales circuit, making a considerable reputation in labour cases. Ten years later he took Silk, the last Q.C. to be appointed by Queen Victoria.

As an M.P. Evans was a prominent radical Liberal closely associated with Lloyd George and, typical of the new Welshman who entered national politics at this time, made the Welsh presence felt on the national stage. An ardent Nonconformist, Evans embraced many of the burning Welsh issues of the two decades before the Great War: temperance, education, tithe reform and disestablishment of the Church. Impetuous, combative and often a bitter critic, he frequently found it difficult to compromise over issues about which he felt strongly. In 1908 Evans was appointed Solicitor General in the Asquith government (Lloyd George became Chancellor of the Exchequer at the same time) but two years later he abandoned his waning political ambitions to accept the Presidency of the Probate, Divorce and Admiralty Division of the High Court. The fire was going out of the old controversies and Nonconformist equality, perhaps the main objective of Welsh radicalism, had lost much of the significance it had held since 1868.

Although certainly competent, his first years as a judge, suggested little of distinction in his work. Evans, however, came into his own during the Great War. Presiding over the Prize Court, and in an area of great complexity, Evans became recognised as a jurist of the first rank, refashioning old doctrines and developing new principles to meet the changed conditions of modern warfare.

A critic once described Evans as 'a lawyer on the make'. Brusque and condescending in manner, it has been said, too, that there was 'about him too much consciousness of undoubted ability to make him attractive to strangers'. Jehu Junior saw in him 'that aloofness of attitude which came of a sense of superiority to men for whom fortune has not made the fight so easy', and felt that he lacked 'the power to appreciate the powers of others'. Yet F. E. Smith, no less, thought that had Evans remained in politics he would have become not only Lord Chancellor but a very great one.

Vanity Fair: 12 February 1908. Leslie Ward.

Sir Watkin Williams Wynn by 'Spy', Vanity Fair *14 June 1873*

Richard John Lloyd Price by 'Spy', Vanity Fair *10 October 1885*

Sir George Osborne Morgan by 'Spy'. Vanity Fair *17 May 1879*

Lewis Llewelyn Dillwyn by 'Spy', Vanity Fair *13 May 1882*

James Keir Hardie by 'Spy', Vanity Fair *8 February 1906*

David Lloyd George by 'Spy'; Vanity Fair *13 November 1907*

John Humffreys Parry by 'Spy', Vanity Fair *13 December 1873*

Sir Roland Bowdler Vaughan Williams by 'Quiz' (John Page Mellor), Vanity Fair
13 December 1890

Sir Samuel Thomas Evans by 'Spy', Vanity Fair *12 February 1908*

Henry Austin Bruce, Lord Aberdare by 'Ape', Vanity Fair *21 August 1869*

Sir William Robert Grove by 'Spy', Vanity Fair *8 August 1887*

Edward Gordon Douglas-Pennant, Lord Penrhyn by 'Spy', Vanity Fair *25 March 1882*

Sir George Elliot by 'Spy', Vanity Fair *29 November 1879*

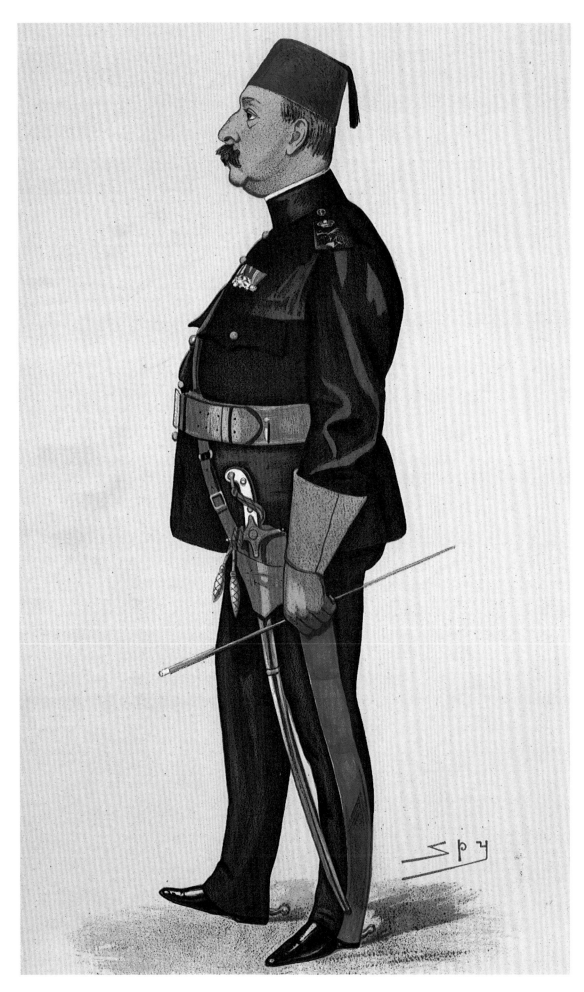

Field Marshal Lord Grenfell by 'Spy', Vanity Fair *19 October 1889*

Education and Arbitration

The years of *Vanity Fair* were years which saw the conversion of England and Wales into school-taught and literate nations, and in Wales, in particular, education was one of the major issues that dominated politics over the last two decades of the century.

For most of the century educational provision in Wales had been lamentably inadequate and little was available to children above the most elementary level. The 'Blue Books' of 1847, despite their attacks on the Welsh language as an obstacle to enlightenment, did serve the useful purpose of drawing public attention to the low level of education and, indeed, of literacy throughout Wales.

Thirty years later, however, there had been little enough change. Although some improvement had been made at the elementary level this lay largely in terms of Church Schools. The establishment of non-denominational schools had lagged behind largely because of Voluntaryist opposition to state grant-aid. This opposition was waning by the time of Forster's Education Act of 1870 but the impact of the provisions of that Act naturally took some years to begin to be really felt.

Above the elementary level Wales was very poorly catered for. In 1880, following parliamentary pressure by Welsh Members at Westminster, a Departmental Committee under the chairmanship of Lord Aberdare was set up to enquire into intermediate and higher education in the Principality. The Committee found that only some four and a half thousand children in Wales enjoyed any grammar or private school education at secondary level and that Nonconformists were especially badly provided for.

In terms of higher education, apart from the limited avenues to Oxford and Cambridge, only St. Davids College, Lampeter, essentially a theological college for the Church, the Normal College at Bangor and the young Aberystwyth College, existing precariously in the face of mounting debts, were available.

The Rev. Henry Arthur Morgan by 'Hay', Vanity Fair *26 January 1889. Henry Morgan was the brother of George Osborne Morgan. Equally brilliant academically but of a totally different political persuasion Morgan, the son of the Vicar of Conwy, was typical of the Welsh middle-class entrant to Oxbridge in the nineteenth century.*

The example of Ireland had been important in the agitation for an enquiry into the state of education in Wales, for Irish education at all levels had benefited from financial support from the government. As a result of the Aberdare Committee's report, a network of secondary schools, subsidised by the government, was established throughout Wales, although this was not to be until 1889 under the terms of the Welsh Intermediate Education Act. Exchequer grants were also made available to two new colleges of higher education – one in South Wales and one in the north. To these – Cardiff and Bangor – was eventually added Aberystwyth, the future of which was assured when it was given government grant-support in 1885. It was not until Gladstone's last ministry, though, in 1893, that the University of Wales came into being on a federal basis.

The Hon. George Thomas Kenyon by 'Spy', Vanity Fair 29 December 1888. Kenyon, Conservative member for Denbigh Boroughs from 1885 to 1895 and from 1901 to 1906, was largely responsible for the passing of the Welsh Intermediate Education Act. In addition to his particular interest in education he typified the landowner with industrial interests and was closely involved in the development of the Wrexham area.

By the 1890s, with the introduction of free elementary education and the gradual adoption throughout Wales of the provisions of the Welsh Intermediate Education Act, an educational edifice had been built far in advance of that in England. Nevertheless, sectarian problems were still to dog the educational scene and were to remain parliamentary issues into the early years of the twentieth century. It was not until the foundation of the Welsh department of the Board of Education in 1907 that the situation began to be finally defused and that, educationally, the people of Wales began to be truly united.

HENRY AUSTIN BRUCE, LORD ABERDARE
(1815-1895)

Born in Aberdare and educated at the Swansea Grammar School, Henry Austin Bruce is best remembered today for his life-long interest in education and especially for his efforts to advance higher education in Wales in the latter part of his life.

Bruce, landowner and coal owner with an interest in the Merthyr iron industry, began his career as a lawyer and was called to the Bar in 1837. His legal career was cut short by ill-health but he returned to public life as stipendiary magistrate for Merthyr Tydfil and Aberdare before being elected as Member of Parliament for Merthyr in 1852. A conservative Liberal, he served as Under Secretary of State at the Home Office from 1862 to 1864 and later as Vice-President of the Committee of the Council for Education under Palmerston and Russell. Bruce's obvious capacity marked him out for high office. Nevertheless, despite his local influence as an industrialist with a liberal outlook and, although a churchman, his recognised Nonconformist sympathies, Bruce lost his seat in 1868 to Henry Richard in the face of the latter's emotional eloquence and Liberationist organisation and the radical traditions of the local electorate.

Bruce was found a seat in Renfrewshire in 1869 and joined the Gladstone cabinet as Home Secretary – 'heaven born' as the Prime Minister described him. For nearly twenty years, commented the *Times* 'no cabinet had included ability so great and so various'. Some time before his death Palmerston had said that whenever Gladstone 'gets my place, we shall have strange doings'. During the next five years a legislative programme of vast, far-reaching reforms shattered the leisurely calm of Parliament. Irish disestablishment, civil service and army reform, education, and the introduction of the secret ballot were all part of a reforming drive which laid the foundations of the modern state.

Among the galaxy of talent in Gladstone's first cabinet Bruce was a worthy rather than a brilliant figure. To 'Jehu Junior' he was 'a feeble official-minded politician . . . [who should never have been] . . . permitted to undertake functions requiring the continual exercise of free and capable judgement'. 'Bruce', concluded 'Jehu Junior', 'is an industrial official and a faithful disciple to Mr. Gladstone [who] . . . has gained credit by converting himself to the ballot; he would gain greater credit by converting himself into an Ex-Secretary of State for the Home Department.' Despite *Vanity Fair*'s strictures and the continuing criticism of his legislative programme Bruce retained his difficult office for four years.

As Home Secretary Bruce was most closely identified with the reform of the licensing laws. His original bill, reintroduced in 1872 in a milder form, sought to achieve a compromise between the hardly reconcilable view of the temperance supporters of the government on the one hand and the liquor trade and brewing interests on the other. While it may have been barely adequate for the temperance movement, the final act alienated the publicans and the brewers – hitherto, with most industrial interests, Liberal in sympathy – and it undoubtedly played no little part in the party's disastrous defeat in 1874. As Gladstone himself was to complain, 'we have been borne down in a torrent of gin and beer'.

In 1873 Bruce was made Lord President of the Council by Gladstone, and raised to the peerage as Lord Aberdare. Within five months, though, the government had fallen and Bruce's official political life had come to an end.

Although Bruce now retired from an active political career he remained prominent in public life. In 1881 he became Governor of the Royal Niger Company and took a close interest in West African affairs. When the Company was, in due course, taken over by the government, Lord Salisbury paid a handsome tribute to Bruce's capacity in conducting its responsibilities and in preserving Britain's influence in the vast areas under its control.

Bruce's main interest in his later years, however, was the advancement of education, especially in Wales. In 1880 Gladstone set up a Departmental Committee to examine intermediate and higher education in Wales and Monmouthshire. Bruce, who had suggested the enquiry, was appointed chairman and acted with speed and efficiency. Within a year (August 1881) the Committee's report was published. Hailed as 'the educational charter of modern Wales', it was a radical document proposing the creation of a new system of intermediate schools in Wales and the setting up of two new colleges of higher education, one in North Wales and one in the south. By 1884 the two new colleges had been established, at Cardiff and Bangor, alongside the Aberystwyth College, still functioning with growing public support, although the creation of Bangor had postulated its death. It was not until 1889, however, that the proposals regarding intermediate education – the essential linchpin of the whole educational strategy – were given serious attention by the government in the Welsh Intermediate Education Act. By that year and on the basis of the Aberdare report a new and coherent educational system was fast being set up in Wales far in advance of that in England.

In 1883 Bruce was chosen as the first President of the new South Wales College. At his installation he made clear his ambition to see the framework of Welsh education crowned by the creation of a University of Wales. He lived to see this hope realised and to be chosen as the first Chancellor of the University. Unhappily, Bruce died a fortnight later.

Vanity Fair: 21 August 1869. Carlo Pellegrini.

THE ARBITRATORS

The report of the Aberdare Committee, in the face of an 'almost unanimous expression in favour of the establishment of provincial colleges', recommended that two colleges of higher education should be set up in Wales, one in North Wales and the other in the south. The South Wales College, the report suggested, should be sited in either Cardiff or Swansea, but was not drawn as to preference. 'Cardiff, and the places within reach of it, supply, within a given area, the larger population, while Swansea and its neighbourhood are the seats of more varied industries'. Memorials in support of their cases were submitted by both towns to Earl Spencer, the Lord President of the Council, but Spencer, who was also Irish Viceroy, had weightier matters on his mind and left the problem of the South Wales College to A. J. Mundella, the Vice-President of the Committee of Council on Education.

Faced by the unyielding hostility of the two towns to one another, Mundella suggested that the College's location could be determined only by arbitration, a device for settling disputes that he had himself introduced into the British hosiery industry twenty years before. Swansea proposed that the matter should be settled by a judicial tribunal, but this idea was not acceptable to Cardiff, which wanted Mundella himself to adjudicate. Eventually, a compromise solution was agreed by the setting up of a three-man arbitration panel under Lord Carlingford, the Lord Privy Seal, as Chairman, together with Mundella and, at the suggestion of Swansea, Lord Bramwell, a former Lord Justice of Appeal, who knew Wales well. In March 1883 they gave their verdict to Cardiff.

A difficult problem had been successfully resolved. It was only natural, therefore, that the arbitrators should be invited to tackle the question of the site of the North Wales College. This was potentially an even more thorny problem because of the question of the future of the Aberystwyth College in the face of the unwillingness of North Wales to accept it as the regional college for the area, the complicating fact that thirteen other towns had entered the lists and the emotive heat of the debate that had thus far developed. In a shorter time than anyone could have imagined, however, the arbitrators came down on the side of Bangor. 'Decidedly the best place in North Wales' Lord Aberdare immediately confided to Mundella.

ANTHONY JOHN MUNDELLA (1825-1897)

Education and Arbitration

The son of an Italian political refugee, and born in Leicester, A. J. Mundella claimed Welsh descent through his mother. After some very elementary schooling, he was apprenticed to a firm of hosiery manufacturers at the age of eleven, but through his abilities he rose to become a factory manager within eight years. Entering into partnership in a hosiery firm in Nottingham in 1849 he remained in business until he had sufficiently established himself to be able to devote his energies to public life.

Mundella first became prominent in local politics as a radical campaigner for the extension of the franchise, the pacification of Ireland and a supporter of free trade. Conscious also of his own early struggles and the responsibilities of an employer to his workforce, Mundella early recognised the necessity of a public system of both elementary and technical education and a reform of industrial relations. In 1866 he established the Nottingham Board of Conciliation and Arbitration in an attempt to improve labour relations at a very difficult time in the hosiery industry. Mundella's scheme was successful and was soon copied elsewhere in Britain and abroad. His success in this area also led to his election as Member of Parliament for Sheffield in 1868, a seat he was to hold for the rest of his life. His energies were devoted to labour reform and especially to the systemisation of public education. In 1874 he introduced his first bill, aimed at reducing the hours worked by child labour in textile mills and increasing the minimum age of employment. Although the bill was unsuccessful it did influence Cross's Factories Act later in the year which achieved most of Mundella's objectives.

Mundella was an ardent advocate of university extension and was a key force in the creation of Firth College in Sheffield (now Sheffield University) as the prototype of the technical colleges which he felt that Britain had to have if it was to maintain its industrial competitiveness in the world. As an advocate of publicly managed elementary education, he was a warm supporter of Forster's Education Act of 1870, but his vision of compulsory elementary education was not fully achieved until his own efforts as Vice-President of the Committee of Council on Education in 1880. Mundella was the driving force behind the educational policy of the Gladstone government of 1880 to 1885 which very much followed his lead. The education code of 1882 and the reorganisation of the schools inspectorate at the same time were both due to his initiatives.

Appointed President of the Board of Trade in 1886, he embarked upon the reform of industrial relations but had to abandon the work that had already resulted in the formation of the Labour Department when the government fell four months later. Back at the Board of Trade in 1892 Mundella resumed his work to strengthen the Labour Department. Having played a successful role in the arbitration that led to the settlement of the coal strike of 1893, he began to press for legislation on arbitration in industrial disputes. His governmental career, however, came to an untimely end in 1894 when he resigned, as a matter of honour, following the institution of a public enquiry, under Lord Justice Vaughan Williams, into the affairs of the New Zealand Loan Company, of which Mundella had previously been a director. No blame attached to him, and, returned unopposed to the House in the 1895 election, so disastrous for the Liberals elsewhere, he was invited to sit on the opposition front bench, devoting his remaining few years to educational reform, serving as Chairman of a Departmental Committee on poor-law schools and taking an active part in the Education Bills of 1896 and 1897.

'Jehu Junior' summed up Mundella as a man who 'understands the working man much as the working-man understands himself . . . He also understands the capitalist . . . and he would abolish at once Ignorance and Strikes by Education and Arbitration . . . '

Vanity Fair: 9 December 1871. J. J. Tissot.

CHICHESTER SAMUEL PARKINSON-FORTESCUE, LORD CARLINGFORD (1823-1898)

He married Lady Waldegrave and Governed Ireland

A scholar of some distinction, Carlingford devoted his life to politics. A decided Liberal, he sat for County Louth from 1847 until his defeat in the general election of 1874 and held government office during the confusing politics of the 1850s and 1860s. Appointed Chief Secretary of Ireland in the short-lived final administration of Lord Russell, he was re-appointed to this office by Gladstone in 1868.

Carlingford, throughout his career, was a strenuous supporter of religious freedom and of conciliation over the problem of Ireland, which he knew intimately. Under Gladstone, Carlingford was almost solely responsible for the two major Irish reforms of the government, the disestablishment of the Irish Church and the Land Act of 1870, although Gladstone, who steered the necessary legislation through the Commons, gained most of the credit. An amiable and courteous man, Carlingford was not thought strong enough to deal with the Irish difficulties that developed after 1870 and was removed to the Board of Trade.

Elevated to the Lords in 1874, he served as Lord Privy Seal and then as Lord President in Gladstone's administration of 1880 to 1885. In both offices he was much involved with education, and especially the problem of the continuation of the Aberystwyth College. Still deeply concerned with the Irish problem, he had a key role in steering the government's policy in Ireland through the Lords, particularly the second Irish Land Act of 1881. Although a conciliator, however, he would not go as far as home rule and ended his political career as a liberal unionist estranged from his old leader.

Vanity Fair: 14 August 1869. Carlo Pellegrini.

SIR GEORGE WILLIAM WILSHERE BRAMWELL, LORD BRAMWELL (1808-1892)

The Exchequer

Embarking initially on a banking career, Bramwell, at the age of twenty-one, went abroad to seek his fortune. Not finding it, he returned home, decided upon the law and, in 1838, was called to the Bar. Acquiring a substantial junior practice and a reputation as a lawyer of solid learning – as *Vanity Fair* says 'he plodded at his work . . . [and] did not seem, therefore, marked out for distinction' – he took Silk in 1851. As a member of a series of commissions, Bramwell was active in promoting the development of a modern approach to both legal procedures and company law, including the introduction of 'limited liability'. In 1856 Bramwell was raised to the judiciary where, noted 'Jehu Junior', 'he is often severe in his sentences . . . and he is especially ready at testing analogies and the adventurous dexterities of the Bar'. Bramwell, known as 'Taffy' was, in fact, one of the strongest judges that ever sat on the bench and was well-known in Wales. He was Swansea's choice for the South Wales arbitration tribunal although his appointment to that for North Wales was greeted with reserve because of an unsubstantiated story about comments he had made about a jury at the Bala Assize. Bramwell was appointed a lord justice of appeal when the Court of Appeal was established in 1876 and, following his retirement, was raised to the peerage six years later. 'For the strength and clearness of his understanding', says his biographer, 'he had few equals on the bench.' Bramwell's brother was an equally distinguished expert witness. After listening to the diametrically opposed opinions of expert witnesses in one case Bramwell is said to have expostulated 'Liars, damned liars, expert witnesses, and then, of course, there is always brother Edwin'.

Vanity Fair: 29 January 1876. Leslie Ward.

DR. CHARLES JOHN VAUGHAN (1816-1897)

Nolo episcopari

Educated at Rugby, under Dr. Thomas Arnold, and at Trinity College, Cambridge, Vaughan was elected a Fellow of his college in 1839. He had a brief flirtation with the law but decided to enter the Church and in due time became vicar of his father's old parish in Leicester. In 1844 he was appointed headmaster of Harrow. The school was then at a low ebb, its numbers low and its discipline in a sorry state. As his biographer tells us, 'within two years Vaughan had raised the numbers to over two hundred, and poured fresh life into the studies and discipline of his pupils. During the last dozen years of his rule it is probable that no school stood higher than Harrow'.

Nevertheless, 'the modern schoolmaster', stressed 'Jehu Junior', 'is expected to know everything, to be able to form his pupils' minds at will, to diffuse an all persuasive benevolence in his waking and sleeping hours. If it were not for the holidays, which are long, few men could stand it. Dr. Vaughan,

though appointed when under thirty, could only endure it for fifteen years'. It was indeed after fifteen years of distinguished service that Vaughan, in the face of a dumbfounded public, suddenly resigned his headmastership in 1859. Almost immediately he was offered the bishopric of Worcester by the Prime Minister, Lord Palmerston. Vaughan declined the preferment, however. A few months later he was offered the bishopric of Rochester. This time Vaughan accepted, but within a few days he changed his mind and withdrew his acceptance. Ely and other sees were also suggested to Vaughan over the next few years, it seems, but always his answer was firmly in the negative. Towards the end of 1860, however, he was appointed vicar of Doncaster, and he entered into the obscure and ordinary work of a parish priest. While at Doncaster Vaughan perfected his powers as a preacher 'of the most eloquent and persuasive order, gentle, earnest, scholarly, tolerant' and embarked upon the most distinctive and influential work of his life, that of training men for the ministry. Establishing a considerable reputation, Vaughan became almost a cult figure for ordinands of the highest quality.

When asked why he had refused to become a bishop Vaughan replied, it is said, because 'I was afraid of ambition'. In the eyes of the world he was seen as an exemplar of Christian humility, 'the one living instance of *nolo episcopari*, who refused bishoprics one after another to hold upon his quiet way'.

The truth, in reality, was very different. Vaughan, as headmaster of Harrow, had had at least one homosexual affair with a pupil and had been exposed by the young John Addington Symonds, by no means a paragon of virtue himself, to his father. The elder Symonds's reaction had been immediate and implacable. Provided Vaughan straightway resigned his headmastership and sought no further preferment in the Church, Symonds would not expose him publicly. Despite appeals from Vaughan's family Dr. Symonds was intractable and for the next twenty years Vaughan went into the wilderness.

It was only in 1879, some years after Dr. Symonds's death, that Vaughan at last felt free to accept preferment to the deanery of Llandaff. Here his public reputation, his apparent Christian character and his obvious freedom from sectarian bias soon won him a unique position in religious and educational circles in South Wales. He took a leading part in the promotion and foundation of the University College at Cardiff and in recognition of his services to the College he was elected its President in 1894.

'No living man', said the archbishop of Canterbury, 'has laid the Church of England under a greater obligation'. That obligation might have been immeasurably greater if it had not been for Vaughan's act of ruinous folly so early in what might have been a career of the utmost distinction.

Vanity Fair: 24 August 1872. Charles Auguste Loye.

SIR WILLIAM ROBERT GROVE (1811-1896)

Galvanic Electricity

Even among the Victorians it is unusual to find a man with the breadth of abilities to achieve great distinction in both science and the law. William Grove was born in Swansea and was educated as a private pupil at the Grammar School. On graduating from Oxford he entered the law and was called to the Bar in 1835. His legal career was impeded by ill-health but this enabled him to follow his natural bent towards science, which had early been encouraged by an amateur Swansea scientist, Benjamin Hill of Clydach. His pioneering work in the new field of electro-chemistry and his development of the gas-voltaic battery, 'the evil-smelling battery that bears his name', were the foundation of his reputation as a scientist. As an active Fellow of the Royal Society, to which he was elected in 1840 at the age of twenty-nine, he regularly contributed papers to its Transactions and, as a 'young Turk', played a central role in the movement to secure the professional reorganisation of the Society to admit only 'cultivators of science' in 1847. In that year he was awarded the Society's medal and was also appointed to the Chair of experimental philosophy at the London Institution.

Grove's scientific distinction began to bring him briefs in patent cases and, as his health improved, he returned fully to the Bar. He took Silk in 1853 and for some years he worked on the South Wales and Chester circuits. 'Mr. Grove's career was rendered brilliant', said 'Jehu Junior', 'first by galvanic electricity, and later by scientific exposition of the law on behalf of commercial clients'. No doubt it was Grove's scientific reputation that led him to be briefed for the defence in the trial of William Palmer, the Rugeley poisoner, in 1856. A member of the Royal Commission on the law of patents, Grove was appointed a Judge of the court of Common Pleas in 1871 and transferred to the Queen's Division in 1880. Although an efficient judge and, although, like so many other Welsh jurists, he achieved success in a variety of areas, Grove made little impact on the bench. To 'Jehu Junior' Grove 'might have been a better Judge had he been made one earlier in life, but it is no fault of his that this was not the case. He has always been noted for his industry, and for an amount of imperturbable good humour which has made him a general favourite with the Bar, and kept him so, even when his faculties had become slow and his science old-fashioned'. It must be said that Grove's legal career robbed science of a very able research chemist. On his retirement from the judiciary at the age of seventy-six, Grove resumed his scientific studies with unabated zeal, although it is clear that his best work and the work on which his scientific reputation was based was that which he had done so long before.

Much of Grove's life was based on London, but he always kept up his Swansea connections, especially with scientific friends like John Dillwyn Llewelyn who, on his lake at Penllergaer, gave what is thought to be the first public demonstration in Britain of an electrically propelled boat – powered by a Grove battery developed by another friend, Benjamin Hill.

William Grove was knighted in 1872 and was made a Privy Councillor in 1887 on his retirement from the bench.

Vanity Fair: 8 October 1887. Leslie Ward.

Industry and Commerce

Britain's status as a nineteenth-century power was firmly based upon its industrial and commercial position which sprang from a combination of technological innovation, natural resource, capital and enterprise. Wales was an important constituent in the nation's industrial and manufacturing power base and it was in South Wales that the Pricipality's most spectacular developments were seen.

Coal was the key to these developments. The richness of the South Wales seams and their proximity to the sea provided the basic resource necessary for the smelting of metals and the commercial outlets required for the marketing of the resulting products. Iron had been one of the earliest heavy industries to be established in South Wales, in the Merthyr area, but in the nineteenth century the adoption of the Bessemer converter process and the shift to steel manufacture, with the need to use non-phosphoric ores from abroad, drew the industry to the coast and Cardiff supplanted Merthyr as its centre. Bessemer had published his process in 1856 but it was some years before its general adoption became practicable. Five years after Bessemer's invention, William Siemens had discovered an alternative method of steel manufacture, the open-hearth process. This again had a long period of gestation but, eventually, because its future was tied closely to the tinplate industry the production of Siemens steel in South Wales grew faster than that of Bessemer steel. By 1912 the production of Siemens steel was 1,360,000 tons compared to 328,000 of Bessemer steel.

Sir Henry Bessemer by 'Spy', Vanity Fair
6 November 1880.

Copper had also been one of the early constituents of industrial development in South Wales. During the course of the century some ninety per cent of the copper smelted in Britain came from the Swansea-Neath area and as this industry began to decline after 1890 in the face of foreign competition its place was taken by tinplate. By 1889 there were ninety-six works, mainly around Swansea and Llanelli, producing 547,000 tons of tinplate. Despite set-backs towards the end of the century, when the McKinley tariff drove the industry out of the American market, by the eve of the Great War new markets had been opened up and over 800,000 tons of tinplate were being produced of which 544,000 tons were exported mainly through the port of Swansea. Swansea, too, was the centre of the zinc smelting industry which was producing some seventy five per cent of Britain's capacity at the outbreak of war in 1914. In 1902 the biggest nickel-smelting works in the world were built at Clydach in the Swansea Valley.

It was the coal industry, though, that dominated the Welsh economy in the latter part of the nineteenth century and it was, again, in South Wales that its growth took place on an unprecedented scale. By 1874 the South Wales coalfield was producing over sixteen million tons, virtually a third of Britain's foreign shipments, a capacity which by 1913 had risen to nearly fifty seven million tons. More than a sixth of this production was mined by the sixty collieries of the Rhondda Valleys and the 41,000 men employed in them. The transition from sail to steam in the course of the 1860s added a new home demand, for Welsh coal was found to be best suited to the requirements of the steamships, and by 1885 the Admiralty was using it exclusively. Through the coal industry, and to a lesser degree the metal industries, the South Wales coastal strip by the end of the century had become not merely the commercial centre of Wales but a focal point of the international economy: Cardiff itself grew tenfold in sixty years and had become the 'coal metropolis of the world'.

Industry was not restricted to South Wales, of course. There was a thriving coal industry in Denbighshire and Flintshire, and Caernarfonshire slate accounted, in 1898, for some seventy per cent of British production: Penrhyn and Dinorwic were the largest slate quarries in the world. Already, however, foreign competition and industrial strife were beginning to take their toll.

But it was in the south that the rapid industrialisation and economic change of the second half of the nineteenth century had most effect. In 1891 the population of the Rhondda Valleys had grown some ten-fold over its 12,000 of thirty years previously. Until the 1890s much of the explosive growth of the population of the South Wales coalfield resulted from emigration from the Welsh countryside. This was a factor of the utmost significance for it helped to maintain and foster native culture and language in the industrial and urban communities of the south long after the pattern of population growth changed.

EDWARD GORDON DOUGLAS-PENNANT, LORD PENRHYN (1800-1886)

Slate

In the eyes of *Vanity Fair* – and to very many others besides – Penrhyn and slate were synonymous. Caernarfonshire slate had been first exploited on a large scale by Richard Pennant (1737?-1808), a Liverpool merchant grown rich on the slave trade and West Indian sugar, who had acquired the Penrhyn estates through marriage in 1765. An entrepreneur and improving landlord in the thrusting eighteenth-century mould, his estates passed to a cousin and, eventually, in 1841, through that cousin's daughter, to her husband Edward Gordon Douglas. Douglas, a Scottish aristocrat, assumed the name Pennant on coming into the estates and in 1866 was raised to the peerage as Lord Penrhyn of Llandegai. By 1876 his Welsh estates extended to nearly 45,000 acres: Penrhyn was the largest landowner in Gwynedd and the third largest landlord in Wales; only Sir Watkin Williams Wynn owned more land in the north. The Welsh estates alone were worth £63,000 a year to Penrhyn but this was less than half the income produced for him by the 2,500 men employed at his slate quarries in Bethesda. Penrhyn was a classic example of the nineteenth century landowner-industrialist and, together with a few comparable families, the Pennants brought Caernarfonshire into the mainstream of industrial development.

Penrhyn affectionately known as 'Yr hen lord' was seen by *Vanity Fair* as 'a most reputable, amiable, charitable, trustworthy man . . . fatherly to his tenants and workmen'. Relations with the quarrymen had always been variable but Penrhyn's approach to problems and grievances was a malleable one and in 1874 he accepted the creation of an elective committee of quarrymen which operated in much the same way as a shop steward's committee works today. Nevertheless, the growing politicisation of the workforce, locally rooted and Nonconformist, their demands for union recognition and the paternalistic reactions of the Penrhyn management under the second Lord Penrhyn generated intense frustration, resentment and bitterness which were to lead to the strikes and stoppages of 1897 and 1900.

Lord Penrhyn was Conservative Member of Parliament for Caernarfonshire from 1841 to 1866 but, noted *Vanity Fair* wryly, 'although in the House of Commons for a quarter of a century, he never attempted oratory or invented a policy'.

Vanity Fair: 25 March 1882. Leslie Ward.

SIR GEORGE ELLIOT (1815-1893)

Geordie

Elizabeth Phillips in her *History of the Pioneers of the Welsh Coalfield* tells us that the career of Sir George Elliot was 'one of the most romantic in the annals of industrialism'. Born of humble parentage, near Gateshead, in County Durham, George Elliot by the age of nine was earning his living as a door-boy in the nearby Whitfield Pit. The 'Durham Pit Laddie', as he was fond of calling himself, often reminisced of how he worked fourteen hours a day underground, in the winter months never seeing the light of day. But, as 'Jehu Junior' stressed, 'his natural talents and ambition were not to be contained by a colliery. At seventeen he had taught himself up to a fair proficiency in mathematics, he also taught himself surveying, so that at one-and-twenty he had already attained to the position of overman, and not long after became chief viewer of the pit . . . So well did he thrive, that at six-and-twenty he became himself the part proprietor of a colliery, and subsequently developed into a coal-owner on a large scale . . . Such was his shrewdness and so correct his judgement, that within a few years he became known as one of the richest men in that northern county where riches are most highly valued'.

Elliot is described as a short, thick-set man, 'without attractions either physical or intellectual, but it was remarkable how quickly he gained the confidence of people – not merely that of the collier and mining speculator, but of those engaged in high finance, both of this country and the Continent . . . Easily accessible to the humblest of workers, he was for many years the idol of the Durham Coalfield'.

He was, said 'Jehu Junior', 'simple, unaffected, and cordial, yet without any pretension, so that his manners are good and his companionship is as pleasant as for those who desire to inform themselves it is profitable'.

Elliot was one of the most distinguished mining engineers of his day and a man of abundant energy whose interests were not confined to the Durham and South Wales coalfields alone. Wire rope manufacture was but one additional industrial activity that captured his attention and he was responsible for the making of the Atlantic Cable. He was thoroughly practical, prompt in action, full of suggestion and initiative, and with an uncanny instinct for finding the weak spot in any undertaking. His colliery experience from so early an age fitted him uniquely for the task of helping to frame the Mines Regulation Bill, in which his assistance was of the utmost value to Lord Aberdare. He was also very much involved in the settlement of the great South Wales coal strike of 1871.

In 1864 Elliot established the Powell-Duffryn Steam Coal Company, in which he acquired a part share, and took over general supervision of its collieries in the Aberdare and Rhymney Valleys. Other holdings were quickly added to the company's assets and under Elliot, the mainspring of the Powell Duffryn operations, the foundations were laid of what was to become the largest sale-coal company in Wales. He was chairman of the company from 1886 to 1889, and continued as an ordinary director for some further years prior to his death in 1893. The George Pit in the Aberdare Valley and the Elliot Colliery in the Rhymney Valley were named after him.

Elliot was also instrumental in developing the Pontypridd, Caerphilly and Newport railway to bring coal from the Aberdare, Merthyr and Rhondda Valleys to Newport. The railway, which greatly enhanced the commercial importance of the port, where he had promoted the construction of the Alexandra Dock in 1875, was opened in 1883 but only in the face of fierce opposition from the Bute Estate.

In politics he was a Conservative, though he confessed he knew little of party politics and cared less. His speeches tended rather more to the anecdotal about people he had met and places he had visited – for he was a widely-travelled man – than to any exposition of Conservative philosophy or policy. It has been said that after listening to one of his inconsequential, yet extraordinarily interesting public speeches, a stranger would be puzzled to know whether Elliot was a Conservative or a Liberal. Nevertheless, he was Member of Parliament for North Durham from 1868 to 1885 and for Newport from 1886 to 1893, and in 1874 he was rewarded by Disraeli with a baronetcy for his public services.

Vanity Fair: 29 November 1879. Leslie Ward.

SIR HENRY HUSSEY VIVIAN, FIRST BARON SWANSEA (1821-1894)

Swansea

In the first years of the nineteenth century John Vivian, a Cornish copper master, extended his copper smelting interests to Swansea. He was attracted to the South Wales coast by its natural advantages of good harbourage, proximity by sea to the Cornish mines, and the rich coal deposits which were so essential to the smelting industry. In 1811 John Vivian built the new copper works of Vivian and Sons at Hafod in the lower Swansea Valley, at that time an area of great natural beauty. Gradually his younger son, John Henry Vivian, took control of the Swansea operations and, by dint of an academic and practical training received in Germany, and his natural business acumen and determination, he achieved considerable success as a copper master and a not insignificant reputation as a scientist. On John Henry's death in 1855 control of the family business was taken over by the eldest son, Henry Hussey Vivian, who was to continue his father's work in building up Vivian and Sons into one of the greatest industrial enterprises in the country and earn for Swansea the title of 'metallurgical centre of the world'.

Like his father, Henry Hussey Vivian spent some time studying metallurgy and languages in Germany and France and, after Cambridge, he served a business apprenticeship as manager of the Liverpool branch of Vivian and Sons before becoming manager of the Hafod works in 1845. Vivian's advanced technical background encouraged his development

of original processes for the making of spelter, the extraction of gold and silver from copper and the production of nickel and cobalt. In 1869 he developed a new smelting process for copper itself, but not before he had succeeded in reducing considerably the 'copper smoke' problem that had been denuding the Swansea Valley for more than a century. Through the distillation of the smoke into chemical by-products – notably sulphuric acid – Vivian, was to establish the foundations of Swansea's chemical industry and to play a significant role in the development of the tinplate industry.

Like his father, too, Vivian was deeply involved in public affairs and was also an M.P. (successively for Truro, Swansea, and, after 1885, Swansea District), but he played a far more active role in the national arena. A Gladstonian reformer, he was not wholeheartedly in sympathy with the Welsh radical movements of the 1880s. In economics he was declared a free trader, in politics a supporter of franchise reform and the secret ballot but his paternalistic approach to his own business interests allowed him little sympathy with the embryonic labour movement. Although an Anglican, he espoused the cause of disestablishment, for Nonconformity, he thought, had saved Wales from infidelity. But on the administrative front he had little time for home rule either in Wales or Ireland. 'Jehu Junior' commented that Vivian 'speaks well and ably on the subjects he understands, and, as he dislikes speaking on any others, he rarely addresses the House . . . He calls himself a sound Liberal, yet he is a gentleman'.

Vivian's special public interest was education, and he took the lead in Parliament over both intermediate and higher education in Wales. In Swansea he encouraged the university movement in the 1880s and spoke for the town in the Cardiff-Swansea arbitration. Although the decision went to Cardiff he became the new South Wales College's first treasurer and later Vice-President. The foundation of the technical school in Swansea in 1895 owed much to his enthusiasm and to his life-long realisation of the benefits to industry of a technical education.

Vivian's heart was in Swansea and its late nineteenth-century commercial developments: the expansion of harbour facilities, the promotion of the Rhondda and Swansea Bay railway to facilitate the transport of valley coal to the town; not least, though, was his advocacy of open spaces. To *Vanity Fair* Vivian had acquired for himself at Swansea 'a popularity and an importance which he owed, not to faith, but to works. He has endowed Swansea with docks, Volunteers, and other industries of a varied kind, and, having endeavoured unsuccessfully to endow it with a college, Swansea has erected a statue to him in his lifetime, a rare honour which he shares with Julius Caesar of Rome and Sir Henry Edwards of Weymouth'.

As a coal owner Vivian was instrumental in introducing the 'sliding scale' for miners' wages after the South Wales coal strike in 1889. In that year he became Chairman of the newly-created Glamorgan County Council. Created a baronet in 1882, he became Lord Swansea eleven years later. A reserved man, like his father, Hussey Vivian concealed his lack of assurance beneath a somewhat pompous and self important exterior – well brought out by 'Spy' in his cartoon.

Vanity Fair: 5 June 1886. Leslie Ward.

SIR JOHN JONES JENKINS, LORD GLANTAWE
(1835-1915)

Known as 'Swansea's Optimist' John Jones Jenkins was born at Clydach in the Swansea Valley. The son of humble parents, he entered the Upper Forest Tinplate Works in Morriston at fifteen and by the age of twenty-three had been appointed out-door manager. In 1859 he became chief partner of the Beaufort Tinplate Works in Morriston and ten years later gave up his partnership having taken over the Swansea Tinplate Company at Cwmbwrla. In 1883 he acquired the Cwmfelin Tin Plate Company. A devoted educationalist, he had started singing classes and a library at the Upper Forest Works. A zealous advocate of the Free Library Scheme, he was also intimately involved in the movement to establish a South Wales college in Swansea. Three times mayor of Swansea (1869/70; 1879/80 and 1880/81), he played a key role in securing Landore as the site for the Siemens Steel Works. Jenkins's business interests were not restricted to the production of tinplate and steel, however. He was very concerned with the development of the docks in Swansea and served as Chairman of the Swansea Harbour Trust from 1891 to 1897. Knighted in 1881, Jenkins was Liberal Member for the Carmarthen Boroughs from 1882 to 1886 – he had considerable tinplate interests in Llanelli – and (as a Liberal Unionist) from 1895 to 1900. He was created Lord Glantawe in 1906 for his public service and staunch Unionist support.

Vanity Fair saw Jenkins as 'one of the very few men living who has had the distinction of sitting in the House of Commons as a Unionist representative of a Welsh constituency . . . he now [as Lord Glantawe] gives expression to the feelings and opinions of that section of his fellow-countrymen who, though large in numbers, would, but for the existence of the House of Lords, be voiceless and practically without influence'. Its description of him as 'sympathetic and tactful' is brought out in his social portrait – no caricature this. Jenkins was the epitome of what *Vanity Fair* required of its heroes. 'He is a believer in early rising and has usually done a good deal of work before other people are out of bed. In spite of a strenuous life, he has retained the detached, meditative urbanity of the recluse. He is a quiet optimist, who has found his philosophy of life serves him well, and his favourite saying is one of Bossuet's – 'God does not always refuse when he delays. He loves perseverance and grants it everything''.'

Vanity Fair: 16 November 1910. WHO

Exploration and the Empire

Victoria, the Queen-Empress by Jean-Baptiste Guth, Vanity Fair *17 June 1897 (Diamond Jubilee Number).*

At the time of Queen Victoria's Diamond Jubilee in 1897, it was estimated that nearly 400 million people in five continents owed their allegiance to the British Crown. The British Empire comprised some thirteen million square miles. France was next with nearly four million square miles and over fifty-six million people, and Germany third with one million square miles and over fourteen million people. The bulk of the territorial aggrandizement which had resulted in these geographical statistics occurred in the decade or so from 1884 and most of the new possessions acquired by the European powers came in the 'scramble for Africa', which was the principal phenomenon of these years. It had been in 1872 that Disraeli, who years before had advocated the abandonment of Britain's overseas 'colonial deadweights', declared that 'England has outgrown the Continent of Europe. England is the metropolis of a great maritime Empire extending to the boundaries of the farthest Ocean.' He was to encapsulate his theory in practice three years later by his purchase of the majority interest in the Suez Canal and in 1876 by the bestowal on the Queen – not a universally popular act – of the title of Empress of India.

The vision of Imperialism had been given birth and a seemingly infinite array of explorers, adventurers and overseas administrators were to glamourise the reality of the vision. Symbols of the virtues of Victorian manhood, many of these larger than life figures of the Empire provide *Vanity Fair* with some of its most exotic caricatures.

Sir Garnet Wolseley (the original of 'the very model of a modern major-general' in The Pirates of Penzance*) by 'Ape',* Vanity Fair *18 April 1874.*

Vanity Fair flourished during the height of the growth of Empire and in supporting British imperial and colonial policies, the magazine, naturally, lauded the achievements of the Empire builders themselves. The military heroes of the time were also celebrated in similar vein and serving officers of Army and Navy were seen as the bastions of society. But not a few were the ornaments of society, too, and the moustached and elegant military dandies frequenting the drawing rooms of the period provided plenty of scope for the caricaturists' satire in their remarkable record of the defenders of the Empire.

Colonel (later Lt. General) Owen Lewis Cope Williams by 'Ape', Vanity Fair *19 January 1878. Owen Williams and his brother Hwfa – who built Sandown Park racecourse – were the great-grandsons of Thomas Williams of Llanidan, the 'Copper King'. Owen commanded the Royal Horse Guards and was a member of the smart set surrounding the Prince of Wales. As Queen Victoria observed laconically, 'the Williams are a bad family'.*

At a time when service to the Empire was a special duty of the younger sons of the landed gentry, it is not surprising to find representatives of the leading families of Wales among the cavalcade of *Vanity Fair*'s military figures, whether abroad, in the field, or at home in the drawing room.

SIR HENRY MORTON STANLEY (1841-1904)

He Found Livingstone

Immortalised by the words 'Dr. Livingstone, I presume', H.M. Stanley, adventurer and explorer, is synonymous with the opening up of the continent of Africa.

Born in Denbigh as John Rowlands, he was placed in the St. Asaph union workhouse as an illegitimate child at the age of three. In his teens, after a number of jobs, he worked his passage from Liverpool to America where his only hope was to seek his fortune in a society where his background would be ignored and where there were enormous opportunities for enterprising young men. Following his arrival in New Orleans, his new life began auspiciously when he was adopted by Henry Stanley, a cotton broker.

After the Civil War, in which he distinguished himself by serving on both sides, the newly named Henry Morton Stanley embarked upon a career as a journalist. From his first assignment covering the Indian Wars of the Great Plains, he moved on to become 'danger correspondent' for the New York Herald reporting on the British campaign against the Emperor Theodore in Abyssinia and the insurrection in Crete.

It was the incorrigible proprietor of the Herald, James Gordon Bennet Jnr., who recognised Stanley's talent and dispatched him to Africa with the instruction to find Livingstone, the Scottish missionary and explorer, dead or alive and regardless of the cost. Livingstone had disappeared without trace in central Africa five years earlier on his last mission to explore and 'civilise' the dark continent.

With the immense resources placed at his disposal, coupled with his own aggressive determination, Stanley, the novice African explorer succeeded where other more experienced men had failed. In newspaper terms – his historic scoop and the publication of his adventure travelogue *How I Found Livingstone* – turned Stanley into a popular hero; but perhaps more significantly it marked the beginning of his career as an African explorer.

Whatever Stanley's motives – whether opportunistic, a desire to overcome his lowly origins by striving for popular acclaim and fortune, or simply a yearning for adventure – he exploited his natural talents for publicity and promotion to raise financial support for further expeditions to Africa.

In 1874 he left England on a journey that took him from Zanzibar across central Africa to the Atlantic coast, and he crowned this achievement by becoming the first white man to explore the River Congo. On his return to Europe in 1877 he immediately began to seek support for an expedition to explore the Congo region and discover its secrets. Disraeli, absorbed in the Eastern Question, showed little interest, but support came from Leopold II, King of the Belgians. Stanley's exploration was thus eventually to culminate in the foundation of the Belgian Congo. His final African adventure came in 1886, when he again traversed central Africa at the behest of the British Government to rescue the fabled Emin Pasha. This was to be the last of the great African journeys. Stanley and his fellow explorers had opened the continent to colonisation, development and exploitation. The 'scramble for Africa' had begun and the continent was to be changed forever.

Stanley's exploits as a popular hero had been recognised with the award of the gold medal of the Geographical Society, a knighthood and the gift of a gold and diamond snuff box from Queen Victoria for finding Livingstone. (This snuff box is now in the collections of the National Museum of Wales.) Despite these accolades, and his marriage to Dorothy Tennant of Cadoxton, Neath, Stanley did not receive the social acceptance and respectability he craved. The cruel cartoon, which appeared in *Vanity Fair* in 1872, depicted him as a poseur and reflected the hostility of society towards the low-born, publicity-seeking, aggressive newspaper reporter. He had, moreover, trespassed into a territory reserved for true Victorian gentlemen, that of being a successful explorer. The caption to Stanley's *Vanity Fair* cartoon reads 'He found Livingstone' and this is the reputation he retained in the public imagination. His immense contribution to the exploration of Africa was, in the last resort, to be virtually forgotten among the public at large.

Vanity Fair: 2 November 1872. Charles Auguste Loye.

SIR HENRY BARTLE EDWARD FRERE (1815-1884)

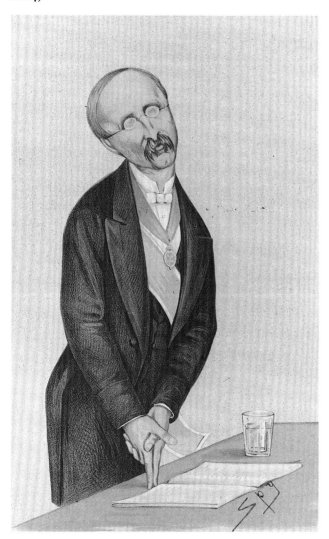

The Slave Trade

Born in the Vale of Clydach in Breconshire, Bartle Frere was to devote his life to public service. He entered the Bombay Civil Service in 1834, where his natural talent for languages, administrative skills and enthusiasm for India ensured his rapid promotion. His first major post came in 1846 when he was appointed as Resident to the Rajah of Sattara and, later, as Commissioner following the annexation – against his advice – of the province as British territory. As Chief Commissioner for Sind from 1850 to 1859, he played a key role in the suppression of the Indian Mutiny. By now an acknowledged authority on Indian affairs, he was appointed a member of the Council of the Governor-General and acted as advisor to Lord Canning as Viceroy of India after the transfer of power from the East India Company to the Crown. His last years in India were spent as Governor of Bombay, and, as a member of the Indian Council had, in the words of Vanity Fair, 'considerable influence upon the attempts to conceive and carry out an intelligible and consistant policy in the East'.

The Foreign Office was very much aware of Frere's abilities and, with widespread public concern over the slave trade in Africa, he was sent to Zanzibar in 1872 to negotiate a treaty with the Sultan to end it. With the idea of establishing a confederacy of territories under British rule in South Africa, Frere was appointed by the Government as Governor of the Cape and High Commissioner of Native Affairs in South Africa in 1877. These were very difficult times in South Africa and following heavy – and uninformed – criticism in Britain of Frere's handling of the Zulu War and of relations with the Boers after the annexation of the Transvaal – he had unavailingly urged on ministers the granting to the Boers of self-government under the Crown – he was called home in 1880.

Ill-served by politicians, Frere did not receive in Britain the credit due to him for his unselfish services until after his death. 'Jehu Junior' was prophetic in his biographical sketch. 'On the whole he is a fairly good specimen of that race of Englishmen whose boldness and activity have won and retained for the Empire domination in the East, and who are habitually rewarded with second-rate distinctions.'

Vanity Fair: 20 September 1873. Leslie Ward.

GENERAL SIR CHARLES WARREN (1840-1927)

Born in Bangor, Charles Warren joined the Royal Engineers in 1857. As a surveyor with a passion for archaeology, he found himself assigned for special duties with the Palestine Exploration Fund in 1867 and became engaged in extensive excavations in Jerusalem. However, even as a surveyor, he was not to be excused active service and, like so many of his contemporaries, his fortunes as a soldier largely depended on the outcome of the colonial wars and military expeditions of the period. After completing a survey of the boundary between the Orange Free State and West Griqualand, he found himself commanding the famous Diamond Fields Horse during the suppression of the Kaffir Insurrection of 1877-78 and later commanding part of the Griqualand West Field Force in the Griqua Rising of 1878.

In the Egyptian War of 1882, his unique combination of talents and experience was enlisted to command the expedition to search for the missing Professor Edward Palmer (the oriental scholar sent by Gladstone to influence the Bedouin and secure the Suez Canal from attack by the Arabs) and ultimately to bring his murderers to justice.

As troubles flared in South Africa once more, Warren was appointed to lead a military expedition to Bechuanaland in 1884 to restore order between the natives and Boer immigrants from the Transvaal. Although vested with full military and civil powers to administer the protectorate, he soon found himself in conflict with the Cape Government and despite his success in resolving the disturbances he was recalled home.

His next appointment as Chief Commissioner of the London Metropolitan Police was equally successful at a very difficult time, with public disturbances in the heart of London and the 'Jack the Ripper' murders to contend with, but strained relations with the Home Secretary led to his resignation in 1888. After a period in command at Singapore, and in home appointments providing little scope for his talents, Warren was recalled from the retired list in 1899 to command the 5th Division on the outbreak of war in South Africa. Controversy continued to dog his steps, as he found himself in conflict with his superiors over the retreat at Spion Kop. Warren retained his command of the 5th Division, however, and was involved in the relief of Ladysmith and the supression of the rebellion in North West Cape Colony, Griqualand West and British Bechuanaland.

Warren was a man of many interests: a founder member of the boy scouts, he was also a scientist of distinction – he was elected to the Royal Society in 1884 – and someone who was deeply interested in religious questions. He was, too, an antiquary of no mean ability, and the cartoon by 'Ape' brings out to the full the character of this typical scholar-soldier.

Vanity Fair: 6 February 1886. Carlo Pellegrini.

FIELD MARSHAL LORD GRENFELL
(1841-1925)

General Sir Francis Grenfell, K.C.B.

Professional soldier and Egyptologist, Francis Grenfell was the fourth son of Pasco St Leger Grenfell, the Swansea copper-master. Intended for the army from an early age, he joined the 60th Rifles in 1859. His early progress in the army was slow and his career was undistinguished. He eventually purchased his commission as a captain in the last gazette before purchase was abolished under the Cardwell army reforms in 1871. Three years later, still having made no mark in the service, he decided to leave the army but he was persuaded to accept the offer of aide-de-camp to General Sir Arthur Cunynghame in South Africa. This proved to be the turning point of his military career. The next seven years were spent on active service and were full of incident. In 1875 Grenfell took part in the Diamond Fields Expedition which established British authority over Griqualand West where the Kimberley diamond field lies, in the Kaffir War of 1878 and in the defeat of the Zulus at Ulundi in 1879.

When the first Boer War broke out in 1881 Grenfell was posted to Natal but a year later he was sent to Egypt as Assistant Adjutant General to Sir Garnet Wolseley in the campaign against Arabi Pasha. After the defeat of the Egyptian army at Tel-el-Kebir, Grenfell stayed in Egypt with the permanent garrison. During the attempt by Wolseley to rescue General Gordon, Grenfell commanded the Egyptian army troops at Aswan on the Nile and co-ordinated the communications for the expeditionary force sent to Khartoum. In 1885 Grenfell was appointed Commander-in-Chief, or Sirdar, of the Egyptian Army, and had the task of rebuilding the force after its destruction in 1882. 'No one' commented 'Jehu Junior' 'except the Dervishes has yet regretted his having done so.'

Recalled to the War Office postings in the United Kingdom in 1892, he returned briefly to Egypt five years later to command the British garrison there. Although technically outranking Kitchener, by now Sirdar of the Egyptian army, Grenfell took care not to cramp the latter's style in the Sudan expedition that culminated in the victory at Omdurman. But it was due very much to Grenfell's earlier re-organisation of the Egyptian army that Kitchener was able to achieve the success that he did. After Egypt Grenfell was posted to Malta as Governor and Commander-in-Chief. He was raised to the peerage in 1902 as Baron Grenfell of Kilvey and a year later given the command of the new 4th Army Corps. In 1904 he was appointed Commander-in-Chief in Ireland and promoted to Field Marshal in 1908.

Grenfell was a man of wide and deep sympathies and an Egyptologist of no small attainment who conducted important excavations at Aswan in his off-duty hours. He was also a talented amateur artist who used his skill to advantage in recording the far-flung places to which he was posted. As the title of his barony would sugget he kept his links with Swansea, too, although so much of his life was spent abroad. President of the Royal Institution of South Wales from 1904 to 1906 he presented a number of Egyptian antiquities to its museum including the mummy of the priest Tem-Hor. As a soldier, while he distinguished himself in the small wars of his time, his true *métier* was as an organiser and an administrator. 'Jehu Junior' crudely observed that Grenfell 'has taught the Blacks how to fight, and he had taught England how the Blacks can fight when led by good officers'. *Vanity Fair* was only one observer to recognise that he was 'full of good qualities and popular everywhere'.

Vanity Fair: 19 October 1889. Leslie Ward.

A List of Welsh Caricatures from *Vanity Fair*

The following is a list of those Welshmen or individuals with close Welsh associations who were the subject of Vanity Fair cartoons. The majority of those included were Welshmen by birth although, of course, a number played little part in the life of Wales and owed their reputation to their role on the national stage or even overseas. There are others, like Sir George Elliot or, in another sphere, Lord Haldane, who were not Welsh at all but whose impact on the Principality and its development require their inclusion. For the sake of completeness, too, all Welsh Members of Parliament have been included, even the odd carpet-bagger like Cornelius Warmington. In all over eighty such people appeared in *Vanity Fair* and in the list below an attempt has been made to be as complete as possible. It may be that some individuals have escaped the net and I would naturally be pleased to hear of these. In compiling the list I owe a debt of gratitude to the seminal work of Ray T. Matthew and Peter Mellini.

Llewllyn Archer Atherley-Jones

Llewellyn Archer Atherley-Jones (1851-1929)
Jonesy   24 January 1912   WH

Frederick J. Benson (1876-?)
Swansea Harbour   24 March 1909   WHO

Sir Henry Bessemer (1813-1898)
Steel   6 November 1880   Spy

Sir Frederick Albert Bosanquet (1837-1923)
Bosey   21 November 1901   Spy

Sir George William Wilshere Bramwell, Lord Bramwell (1808-1892)
The Exchequer   29 January 1876   Spy

Henry Austin Bruce, Lord Aberdare (1815-1895)
He has Gained Credit   21 August 1869   Ape

Lieutenant-General Sir William Francis Butler (1838-1910)
A Radical General   9 January 1907   Spy

Spencer Compton Cavendish, Marquess of Hartington, afterwards
  Duke of Devonshire (1833-1908)
His Ability and Industry   27 March 1869   Ape

Colonel William Cornwallis Cornwallis-West (1835-1917)
Denbighshire   16 July 1892   Spy

John Crichton-Stuart, Marquess of Bute (1881-1947)
The Bute   14 April 1910   WHO

Lord Ninian Crichton-Stuart (1883-1915)
Cardiff   13 July 1910   WHO

Lewis Llewelyn Dillwyn (1814-1892)
A Wet Quaker   13 May 1882   Spy

Sir John Talbot Dillwyn Llewelyn (1836-1927)
Swansea   11 October 1900   Spy

Hon. Edward Gordon Douglas-Pennant, Lord Penrhyn (1800-1886)
Slate   25 March 1882   Spy

William Edwardes, Lord Kensington

William Edwardes, Lord Kensington (1835-1896)
A Whip   7 September 1878 Spy

Sir George Elliot (1815-1893)
Geordie   29 November 1879 Spy

Sir Samuel Thomas Evans (1859-1918)
Sam   12 February 1908   Spy

Cyril Flower, Lord Battersea and Overstrand (1843-1907)
The Senator   19 August 1882   T

Sir Henry Bartle Edward Frere (1815-1884)
The Slave Trade   20 September 1873 Spy

Sir Daniel Gooch (1816-1889)
The Great Western   9 December 1882 Spy

Field Marshal Lord Grenfell (1841-1925)
General Sir Francis Grenfell, K.C.B.   19 October 1889   Spy

Sir Arthur Sackville Trevor Griffith-Boscawen (1865-1946)
Housing   14 August 1912   Ray

Sir William Robert Grove (1811-1896)
Galvanic Electricity   8 October 1887   Spy

Hon. Arthur Edward Guest (1841-1898)
A South Western Director   27 August 1896   Spy

Sir Ivor Bertie Guest, Lord Wimborne (1835-1914)
Tennis   23 September 1882 T

Hon. Montague John Guest (1839-1909)
Monty   7 August 1880   Spy

Hon. Thomas Merthyr Guest

Hon. Thomas Merthyr Guest (1838-1904)		
Blackmore Vale	11 November 1897	CG
Richard Burdon Haldane, Lord Haldane (1856-1928)		
A Hegelian Politician	13 February 1896	Spy
Government Marked	19 March 1913	Owl
Hon. Frederick Stephen Archibald Hanbury-Tracy (1848-1906)		
Gentle and Liberal	17 May 1884	Spy
Sir William George Granville Venables Vernon Harcourt (1827-1904)		
He Was Considered an Able Man Till He Assumed His Own Name	4 June 1870	Atn
A retired Leader	11 May 1899	Cloister
James Keir Hardie (1856-1915)		
Queer Hardie	8 February 1906	Spy
Edward George Hemmerde (1871-1948)		
The New Recorder	19 May 1909	Spy
Edward James Herbert, Earl of Powis (1818-1891)		
Mouldy	27 May 1876	Spy
Sir John Jackson (1851-1919)		
Docks and Harbours	29 September 1909	Spy
Sir John Jones Jenkins, Lord Glantawe (1835-1915)		
Swansea	16 November 1910	WHO
Hon. George Thomas Kenyon (1840-1908)		
Denbigh Boroughs	29 December 1888	Spy
David Lloyd George, Earl Lloyd George (1863-1945)		
A Nonconformist Genius	13 November 1907	Spy
Sampson Samuel Lloyd (1820-1889)		
Fair Trade	11 March 1882	Spy

Rev. Joseph Leycester Lyne

Rev. Joseph Leycester Lyne ('Father Ignatius') (1837-1908)
  Father Ignatius   9 April 1887   Ape

General Sir Harry Aubrey de Vere Maclean (1848-1920)
  The Kaid   25 February 1904 Spy

Reginald McKenna

Reginald McKenna (1863-1943)
  In the winning crew   31 October 1906   Spy
  The Universal Puzzle is:
  Find Mr. M'Kenna   23 April 1913   Owl

Hon. Frederic Courtenay Morgan (1834-1909)
  Fred   2 November 1893   Spy

Sir George Osborne Morgan (1826-1897)
  Burials   17 May 1879   Spy

Rev. Henry Arthur Morgan (1830-1912)
  Black Morgan   26 January 1889   Hay

Anthony John Mundella (1825-1897)
  Education and Arbitration   9 December 1871- (Tissot)

Sir George Newnes (1851-1910)
  East Cambridgeshire   31 May 1894   Spy

General Lord Alfred Henry Paget (1816-1888)
  The Clerk Marshal   3 July 1875   Ape

Admiral Lord Clarence Edward Paget (1811-1895)
  Sailor, Politician and Sculptor   25 December 1875 Ape

General Lord George Augustus Frederick Paget (1818-1880)
  A Soldier   13 October 1877   Spy

Henry Paget, Marquess of Anglesey

Henry Paget, Marquess of Anglesey (1835-1898)
  The Head of the Pagets   18 September 1880 Ape

Chichester Samuel Parkinson-Fortescue, Lord
  Carlingford (1823-1898)
  He Married Lady Waldegrave and Governed Ireland   14 August 1869   Ape

John Humffreys Parry (1816-1880)
  A Lawyer   13 December 1873 Spy

Professor Frederick York Powell

Professor Frederick York Powell (1850-1904)
  Oxford Modern History   21 March 1895   Spy

Richard John Lloyd Price of Rhiwlas (1843-1923)
  Pointers   10 October 1885   Spy

Sir John Henry Puleston (1829-1908) *Devonport*	14 October 1882	Spy
Henry Cecil Raikes (1839-1891) *Order, Order*	17 April 1875	Ape
Sir John William Ramsden (1831-1914) *Huddersfield*	28 June 1884	Spy
Sir Edward James Reed (1830-1906) *Naval Construction*	20 March 1875	Ape
Sir John David Rees (1854-1922) *Montgomery District*	20 February 1907	Spy
Sir Rhys Rhys-Williams (1865-1955) *Rhys K.C.*	29 October 1913	Owl

John Roberts, Junior

John Roberts, Junior (1848-?) *The Champion Roberts*	4 April 1885	Ape
Henry Richard (1812-1888) *Peace*	4 September 1880	Spy
Samuel Smith (1836-1906) *Sammy*	4 August 1904	Spy
George Fitzroy Henry Somerset, Lord Raglan (1857-1921) *Under-Secretary for War*	14 February 1901	Spy
Henry Charles Fitzroy Somerset, Duke of Beaufort (1824-1899) *The Duke of Sport* *Badminton*	30 September 1876 7 September 1893	Spy Spy
Sir Henry Morton Stanley (1841-1904) *He Found Livingstone*	2 November 1872	-(Loye)
Rev. Bernard John Vaughan, S.J. (1847-1922) *A Modern Savonarola*	30 January 1907	Spy
Dr. Charles John Vaughan, Dean of Llandaff (1816-1897) *Nolo episcopari*	24 August 1872	- (Loye)
Cardinal Herbert Vaughan, Archbishop of Westminster (1832-1903) *Westminster*	7 January 1893	Spy
Sir Roland Lomax Bowdler Vaughan Williams (1838-1916) *The Mandarin* *A Rustic Judge*	13 December 1890 2 March 1899	Quiz CGD

Victor Albert George Child Villiers, Earl of Jersey (1845-1915)
New South Wales   11 October 1890   Spy

Sir Henry Hussey Vivian, Lord Swansea (1821-1894)
Swansea   5 June 1886   Spy

Sir Cornelius Marshall Warmington (1842-1908)
Directors' Liability   7 February 1891 Stuff

General Sir Charles Warren (1840-1927)
Bechuanaland   6 February 1886 Ape

Sir Arthur Osmond Williams (1849-1927)
The Champion of the Ladies   1 December 1909 H.C.O.

Lieutenant General Owen Lewis Cope Williams (1836-1904)
The Prince   19 January 1878 Ape

Thomas Anthony Hwfa Williams

Thomas Anthony Hwfa Williams (1849-1926)
Sandown Park   7 November 1891 Spy

Charles Watkin Williams Wynn (1822-1896)
Montgomeryshire   28 June 1879   Spy

Sir Watkin Williams Wynn (1820-1885)
The King of Wales   14 June 1873   Spy

Robert George Windsor-Clive, Earl of Plymouth (1875-1923)
Good Works   5 April 1906   Spy
Crystal Palace   31 December 1913 Hic

Windham Thomas Wyndham-Quin, Earl of Dunraven and
    Mountearl (1841-1926)
Active   4 May 1878   Spy

Charles Robert Wynn-Carrington, Marquess of Lincolnshire
    and Baron Carrington (1843-1928)
Charlie   7 February 1874 Ape
Small Holdings   11 September 1907 Spy

Dr. Nathaniel Edward Yorke-Davies (1841-1912?)
Dietetics   12 April 1900   Spy

Select Bibliography

Caricature and *Vanity Fair*

William Feaver, *Masters of Caricature* (London 1981).

Richard Godfrey, *English Caricature, 1620 to the Present* (London 1984).

Ernst H. Gombrich and Ernst Kris, *Caricature* (London 1940).

Eileen Harris, 'Carlo Pellegrini : Man and 'Ape', *Apollo*, vol. 103, no. 167, January 1976, pp. 53-57.

David Low, *British Cartoonists, Caricature and Comic Artists* (London 1942).

David Low, 'The Purpose of Caricature', *The Listener*, 16 August 1933.

Ray T. Matthew and Peter Mellini, *In 'Vanity Fair'* (London, Berkeley and Los Angeles 1982).

B. Fletcher Robinson, 'Chronicles in Cartoons : A Record of Our Times', *The Windsor Magazine*, 1905 – 1906.

Leslie Ward, *Forty Years of 'Spy'* (London 1915).

General

The Dictionary of National Biography (London, Compact Edition 1975).

The Dictionary of Welsh Biography (London 1959).

G. Kitson Clark, *The Making of Victorian England* (London 1962).

G. Kitson Clark, *An Expanding Society: Britain 1830-1900* (Cambridge and Melbourne 1967).

R.C.K. Ensor, *England 1870-1914* (London 1936).

Robert Rhodes James, *The British Revolution : British Politics 1880-1939, vol. 1 : From Gladstone to Asquith 1880-1914* (London 1976).

Kenneth O. Morgan, *Rebirth of a Nation : Wales 1880-1980* (Oxford 1981).

Kenneth O. Morgan, *Wales in British Politics 1868-1922* (Cardiff 1970).

Donald Read, *England 1868-1914* (London 1979).